In Search KITE
OF THE
RUNNER

POPULAR INSIGHTS

Solving the DaVinci Code Mystery
Brandon Gilvin

Wisdom from the Five People You Meet in Heaven
Brandon Gilvin and Heather Godsey

Unveiling the Secret Life of Bees
Amy Lignitz Harken

Gifts of Gilead
Amy Lignitz Harken
Lee Hull Moses

In Search of the Kite Runner
Judi Slayden Hayes

Inside the Red Tent
Sandra Hack Polaski

In Search OF THE KITE RUNNER

Judi Slayden Hayes

CHALICE PRESS
ST. LOUIS, MISSOURI

Bible quotations, unless otherwise noted, are from the *New Revised Standard Version Bible,* copyright 1989, Division of Christian Education of the National Council of the Churches of Christ in the United States of America. Used by permission. All rights reserved.

Scripture quotations marked (NIV) are taken from the HOLY BIBLE, NEW INTERNATIONAL VERSION®. NIV®. Copyright © 1973, 1978, 1984 by International Bible Society. Used by permission of Zondervan Publishing House. All rights reserved.

Page numbers in this book refer to the hardcover edition of *The Kite Runner,* published by Riverhead Boooks in 2003, and differ from other editions.

Cover art: Getty Images
Cover and interior design: Elizabeth Wright

Visit Chalice Press on the World Wide Web at
www.chalicepress.com

10 9 8 7 6 5 4 3 2 1   07 08 09 10 11 12

Library of Congress Cataloging–in–Publication Data

Hayes, Judi.
  In search of the kite runner / Judi Slayden Hayes.
    p. cm.
  ISBN-13: 978-0-8272-3029-3
  1. Hosseini, Khaled. Kite runner. 2. Afghanistan—In literature. 3. Male friendship in literature. 4. Boys in literature. 5. Betrayal in literature. 6. Guilt in literature. 7. Forgiveness in literature. 8. Fathers and sons in literature. 9. Religion in literature. 10. Islam in literature. I. Title.

PS3608.O832K583 2006
813'.6—dc22   2006020513

May 23
Khyber Pass
May 9 : 5+6
May 16 : 7+8

To David, my husband and best friend,
who has read and researched along with me,
and to the women of the newly formed
Like-Minded Wild and Wonderful Women's Book Club—
Jeanie Reynolds, Susan Richardson,
and Teresa Walters—
whose first selection was The Kite Runner,
and my friend, G. B. Howell Jr.,
who read and listened

Contents

Introduction   1

1   Innocence and Responsibility   5

2   Kites   21

3   Afghanistan   27

4   Fathers and Sons, Brothers and Friends   35

5   Islam   55

6   Doing Good, Being Religious   67

7   From Sin and Suffering to Freedom in   83
    Finding Forgiveness

8   Living Life "a Thousand Times Over"   97

Appendix: Online Resources   104

Introduction

For more than ten years Mark Caldwell was my pastor. At the end of almost every Sunday morning worship service, he voiced this benediction: "In the goodness of God we were brought into this world in the first place. By the grace of God, we've been kept every step we've ever taken. And by the love of God, most fully revealed, we believe, in Jesus the Christ, we are being redeemed." That's my context for writing this book. My worldview is Christian and biblical. Having grown up in a Christian home, and having spent my life in churches and Christian publishing, I have no other context for reading and writing about *The Kite Runner*. Other writers have looked at *The Kite Runner* as a sociopolitical comment on the turbulence in Afghanistan. That's really not my purpose in this book, though no serious reader could ignore the impact of the government and power ruling the country, which precipitated the events of *The Kite Runner*. This book looks at it more from a Christian worldview and seeks to draw out implications for Christian readers in their own context.

I also want to establish this book's Christian orientation at the very beginning because it is clearly not the worldview of the storyteller in *The Kite Runner*. His viewpoint is in many ways secular; when it is religious, the perspective is from an Islamic worldview, not a Judeo-Christian perspective. But because Islam, Judaism, and Christianity hold in common at least some of events in the book of Genesis in the Hebrew Bible, we will find much there that informs our reading of *The Kite Runner*.

Often in writing this book, I simply take what Amir, the storyteller, says or does, as it relates to religion, at face value

1

without trying to overanalyze everything to put it in a Christian context. My purpose here is not to confront Islam but to see how my experiences as a Christian and as a human being resonate with what I read in *The Kite Runner*. There I find a great deal to inform my own life without having to criticize or contradict others' religious experiences.

Perhaps one thing that surprised me is how much *The Kite Runner* speaks to all people in much the same way in their deepest needs to deal with their pain and guilt, to find forgiveness, and to do something good or significant with their lives. I had lunch one day with a young friend whose recognized need for organized religion in her day-to-day life is pretty much nonexistent, yet in her life I consistently observe so many good traits that I'm always impressed by the high standards of integrity she maintains in every area of her life. I asked her if she had read *The Kite Runner*. She had, and immediately began to talk about goodness, guilt, and all the ways she attempts to make up for her perceived wrongdoing and resulting guilt. I left that lunch thinking it was sad that she carried around such a load of guilt when she could turn it over to God because of the redemptive work of Jesus, and move on.

The next week, however, I had two experiences with Christian friends, one in the context of discussing *The Kite Runner* and the other a painful talk about his guilt for how his parenting skills may have had a role in his son's addiction and what all of that was doing to his ministry. Both of these Christians talked about doing good to overcome the guilt and pain in their lives. From a Christian perspective they continued to deal with their unworthiness and the need to overcome it, even while believing that they live each day in God's redemptive grace.

My friends have in common the human condition—the loss of innocence, the burden of guilt, the need for redemption. *The Kite Runner* helps us explore those issues and many more.

A novel that can appeal to young and old of different faith perspectives and help us all take a deeper look at the human condition is a novel worth reading. *The Kite Runner* is both a quick-read page-turner *and* a powerful novel that makes a lasting impression and lends itself to hours of thought, self-reflection, and discussion. This book you are currently holding is a result of my thoughts, my self-reflection, and hours of discussion. Although the end result is also based on a good bit of research and additional reading, it still very much reflects my journey in processing this excellent work of fiction. My goal is that it will lead you on your own path to maximize your experience in reading *The Kite Runner*. You will likely find that in addition to my explorations, your reading and reflection will take you in some additional directions. That's part of what makes *The Kite Runner* such an excellent book.

One brief word of warning before you begin reading this book: the approach here is thematic, not chapter by chapter, so it cannot easily be read while you are reading *The Kite Runner*. If you begin this book before completing *The Kite Runner*, some of the twists and turns of the plot may be revealed before you are ready for them. This book will, however, help you reflect on *The Kite Runner* and assist you in guiding group discussions.

CHAPTER 1

Innocence and Responsibility

I became what I am today at the age of twelve, on a frigid overcast day in the winter of 1975.

(*The Kite Runner*, 1)

Although we don't know what this defining moment is in the book for several chapters, everything moves toward it, and everything following is in some way tied to or affected by that defining moment—the rape of Hassan. How many times Amir must have revisited the events of that day in his mind, his best and worst day, his day of victory and of shame—and Hassan was right there in every scene.

The memorable, fateful day began with breakfast, prepared by Hassan. During breakfast Hassan shared a dream in which he and Amir had had a different kind of victory and were revered by all the people. But Amir's response, as was often the case, was to snap at Hassan. Instead of apologizing, he simply thought that Hassan would understand, knowing he was nervous.

The day seemed to be perfect—crisp and clear with a cloudless sky—"blameless blue," a color Amir would not see again for many years. The air was filled with excitement, children filled the streets, rooftops were crowded with adults drinking tea, and the anticipation was palpable. But in spite of the crowd and the excitement and Baba and Rahim Khan looking on—or perhaps because of the latter—Amir was ready to pack up and go home. Only Hassan's calming words, recalling the dream he'd shared at breakfast, reassured Amir and enabled him to go on.

Then finally, after hours of cutting down one kite at a time, Amir finally guided his big kite to cut down the competing big blue kite, the last remaining enemy to be defeated. The moment was surreal, with Amir thinking that he would soon return to his routine life, wanting to please his father and always failing. Then he saw his father, his joy and excitement, and Amir felt approval at last.

> Then I saw Baba on our roof. He was standing on the edge, pumping both of his fists. Hollering and clapping. And that right there was the single greatest moment of my twelve years of life, seeing Baba on the roof, proud of me at last. (*The Kite Runner*, 58)

That moment should have defined the day and provided a lifetime of satisfaction, of one good day, for Amir. But it was not to be. This was the zenith, and Amir would never have guessed that he, like his kite, could soar so high at one moment and plummet so low the next.

Hassan offered to chase the blue kite so that he and Amir would have the tangible trophy to remind them of this momentous day. So off he ran, Hassan, the greatest kite runner of them all. Amir stayed put, retrieved his own kite, and enjoyed the congratulations of the crowd. He took the kite home, handed it to Ali, and went back on the streets to find Hassan and the blue kite. As he searched for Hassan, he anticipated his hero's welcome when he returned. He thought no further. "Then the old warrior would walk to the young one, embrace him, acknowledge his worthiness. Vindication. Salvation. Redemption. And then? Well…happily ever after, of course. What else?" (*The Kite Runner*, 59).

The days of Amir's happily-ever-after would soon be forever ended, and he would just be beginning his lifelong pursuit of vindication, salvation, and redemption.

Did foreboding begin to enter the scene as Amir's search took longer and longer? It was beginning to get dark. A well-wisher stopped to congratulate Amir and to make fun of the Hazara companion for whom he searched. A shopkeeper pointed out that Hassan had no business in that part of town alone at that time of day.

Finally, Amir found Hassan in a deserted place surrounded by bullies he had successfully confronted only days before. Beside them was the blue kite. Amir overheard Assef, the leader of the group, offer to give Hassan his freedom in exchange for the kite. Was the offer sincere or just to taunt Hassan? Hassan, with Amir watching in hiding, was never to know the answer to that question because, in loyalty to his master—and at least in his mind, his friend—he refused to relinquish the kite. So, Assef said, he must punish the Hazara. And Amir watched and did nothing.

> I had one last chance to make a decision. One final opportunity to decide who I was going to be. I could step into that alley, stand up for Hassan—the way he'd stood up for me all those times in the past—and accept whatever would happen to me. Or I could run.
>
> In the end, I ran. (*The Kite Runner,* 68)

It was the end of innocence in Amir's life.

A Literary Comparison

Most people have favorite coming-of-age or loss-of-innocence novels, often those read during their teenage years. It's a popular genre, one that has endured the ages, perhaps because it continually speaks to the human condition. Generational favorites include Mark Twain's *Huckleberry Finn,* Harper Lee's *To Kill a Mockingbird,* and J. D. Salinger's *The Catcher in the Rye.* Often these are written from the male perspective, as is *The Kite Runner,* but there are lesser known parallels from a female perspective, and this is a genre that is growing in popularity today, with prominent examples including Kaye Gibbons's *Ellen Foster,* Ann Brashares's *The Sisterhood of the Traveling Pants,* and Sue Monk Kidd's *The Secret Life of Bees.*

Perhaps a lesser known book will serve well as a comparison to *The Kite Runner. Nashville 1864: The Dying of the Light,* is a short Civil War novel by Madison Jones (Nashville: J. S. Sanders, 1997). It is written in the form of a memoir of the main character, Steven Moore, who experienced the American Civil War as a boy. The context is the Union Army's occupation of Nashville in 1862. Moore, the lead character, wrote his memoir as an adult, writing after thirty-six years about the experiences he had as a twelve-year-old. Dink, his slave and perhaps his friend, who is about the same age, shares the journey. In 1862 Steven's father, Jason Moore, joined the Confederate Army. Before he left home, he took Steven aside and talked with him. He leveled with his son about the danger of war, closing with, "You will have to take the place of a man, Steven, whatever happens" (*Nashville 1864*, 6).

Steven already was a big help to his mother, who preserved the family and the home with an iron will, with only the help of Dink and Dink's father, Pompey. One by one the other slaves had abandoned the farm.

The Moore farm on the edge of Nashville, like the people who lived there, did not immediately feel the impact of the occupation, but the effects worsened over time. The slaves left, the Union Army stole the livestock, food was running out, and finally the severe illness of Steven's younger sister Liza took its toll. The Confederate Army had just been defeated in the Battle of Franklin, and the armies had turned toward Nashville. Almost two years after Jason had left for the war, the family was in despair. Hearing that his father's unit was nearby, Steven, after days of begging, convinced his mother that he and Dink should go find Jason and bring him home in hopes that with him there everything would be better.

Most of the book is about the boys' search for Jason Moore and the experiences they had in seeing what war is really like. On their journey Dink often voiced more wisdom than Steven, wanting to return home. But Steven insisted that they continue to hunt for his father; and Dink, the loyal slave, stayed by his side until the house in which they were resting and hiding was blown up by the Union Army. Steven escaped, but Dink was killed. The memoir of this time recalls Steven's feelings:

> Over the years I have a thousand times in memory profoundly regretted this, my forcing him to go along. Determined though he surely was to go if I did, he was acting against his will in my behalf. No matter the bond

of real affection between us, this was what it meant to be a slave. This fact, of which I was only half unconscious, was the source of my discomfort with the word "slave," and thus was a fact that, more closely examined, might well have led me to a different course of action. I think I could have made him stay in the barn. A couple of days and all harm most likely would have passed him by, leaving him free to go back home or anywhere else he wanted. But I needed him. He was not especially bright or physically resourceful, but he was there, as he had been all my life, a sure and certain strength where it was wanted. So it was that against his will I led him into dangers in no way his to face. (*Nashville 1864*, 56–57)

Steven Moore's defining moment, the death of his slave Dink, would haunt him the rest of his life, much as Amir's life was forever changed and continuously impacted by the rape of Hassan, his servant.

A Biblical Parallel

Many stories in the Bible are filled with relatively young people who have pivotal moments that set the course for the rest of their lives. Among the stories we could consider are the stories of the patriarchs, especially the stories of Esau and Jacob; but we will look at these stories in a later chapter, in which we consider the relationships of fathers and sons. In almost every biblical story of coming of age and loss of innocence, the father plays a prominent role, so these two areas of discussion are not easily segmented. The influence of the father on the son is significant in the story, even if the father did not cause the pivotal event, as in *The Kite Runner*. To choose just one example, let's look at the Old Testament story of Joseph, the son of Jacob, the last of the three patriarchs—Abraham, Isaac, and Jacob. Let's begin the story with Jacob's flight to Haran to live with his uncle Laban after tricking Esau out of his birthright and stealing his father's blessing.

Isaac told Jacob not to marry a Canaanite woman, one who worshiped idols and did not follow the one true God. When Jacob arrived in Haran, he soon fell in love with Rachel, his cousin. He asked Laban for her hand in marriage, and Laban answered that he would have to work for seven years for Rachel. This he did, but Laban tricked him. When the veils came off after the wedding ceremony, Jacob found he was married to Leah, Rachel's older sister. Laban told him he could marry Rachel as well, but would then be obliged to work for Laban another seven years, which he did. Leah had four sons for Jacob, but Rachel had none. So Rachel sent in her maid to him, and she gave Jacob two more sons. Leah's maid also had two sons by Jacob. Then, Leah had two more sons. And then, finally, Rachel had a son, Joseph. He, the only son of the wife for whom Jacob had worked for fourteen years, quickly became the favorite. Later Rachel had another son, Benjamin, but she died giving birth to him.

Joseph often acted more like an only son than one with ten older brothers, and he gave every evidence of being a spoiled brat. He tattled to his father about his brothers. He had a splendid coat with long sleeves that Jacob had made for him, and he wore it proudly in front of his brothers. Joseph, like his father, was a dreamer. He twice dreamed symbolic dreams about his brothers bowing down to him, and he told them about his dreams. His brothers knew he was their father's favorite, and they hated him for it.

When his brothers were out tending sheep in the field, Joseph went to check on them for his father. When they saw him coming, they plotted to kill him; but Reuben talked them out of their plan. They took his coat and threw him into a pit until they could decide what to do. While they were eating, they saw a caravan on their way to Egypt and decided to sell their brother Joseph into slavery. Before they went home, they took Joseph's coat and dipped it in goat's blood. When they took it to Jacob, he assumed that Joseph had been killed by wild animals. And Jacob mourned for his lost son.

Joseph, meanwhile, was sold in Egypt to Potiphar, an official in Pharaoh's court.

Up to this point in the story, Joseph had little control over the events that changed his life, except perhaps his youthful arrogance in front of his brothers and his disregard for their feelings. Now in Egypt, away from his family and their way of living, how he acted was up to him. He was performing well and getting attention from Potiphar when his first test came. Potiphar's wife found him attractive and tried to get him into bed with her. When he repeatedly refused, she grabbed his garment, and he fled without it. Once again his clothing was used against him. She showed the garment to her husband and accused Joseph of attempting to compromise her. When he heard this, Potiphar threw him in jail.

While in prison, Joseph interpreted dreams for the cupbearer and the baker. Joseph told the cupbearer that he would be restored to his position. He explained his innocence and asked the cupbearer to remember him when he got out of prison. But the cupbearer forgot all about Joseph for two more years.

When Pharaoh had dreams that no one could interpret, the cupbearer remembered Joseph. He was brought to Pharaoh and interpreted the dreams. Joseph told Pharaoh that seven prosperous years would be followed by seven years of famine. The dreams were a warning to prepare for the lean years during the prosperous years. Pharaoh rewarded Joseph by putting him in charge of overseeing the preparations for the years of drought and famine.

Joseph was once again tested when his brothers came to Egypt to find food during the years of drought. They did not recognize Joseph. Joseph could have had them killed or let them starve. Instead Joseph forgave his brothers and eventually reunited all of them in Egypt.

Pivotal events in Joseph's life, though not of his own making, ultimately saved his family and began to bring together the Hebrew people, who four hundred years later would leave Egypt, where they eventually had become slaves. At that point they were poised to follow God and become God's chosen people.

Innocence and Responsibility

These three stories—Amir's story in *The Kite Runner,* Steven Moore's story in *Nashville 1864,* and Joseph's story in Genesis— have some things in common with other stories of loss of innocence and coming of age.

A Time of Innocence and a Pivotal Event

Before the pivotal events took place, the three young men lived in relative innocence. Some conflict is evident, building to the event; yet they all live with a purity that will not be restored. Amir's world is one of school and home, movies and kites, friends and bullies, and wanting to please his father. Most of his thoughts are focused on himself: his desire to win the kite-fighting contest; his selfish, self-centered, and sometimes cruel treatment of Hassan. On the same day that his innocence was taken away, he thought the greatest thing in life was a kite-fighting victory that would ensure an ongoing happily-ever-after. He was just beginning to think about some real issues in life, such as what he believed about God and the complex meaning of relationships and friendships, when the fateful day of both victory and defeat changed his life forever. Growing up was no longer gradual. He had suddenly been thrust into adulthood.

Steven was dealing with the absence of his father, his need to be a man at home, his juvenile view of the war, and his assumption that the Confederate Army would be victorious, his father would return, and life would go on as it had before the war. But until he left home, he was largely protected by his mother and Pompey, the faithful old slave. Before he arrived at the battlefield and saw war-weary, starving men and began to get a sense that this was not the war of his daydreams, he had had a romantic notion of joining the army in a few months, getting back at the Yankees for disrupting his life, and coming home with the other soldiers in victory to a hero's welcome. The death of Dink combined with the reality of war to be the pivotal point in his life.

Joseph, his father's favorite son, had a life of relative indulgence before his brothers shipped him off to Egypt. In arrogance and innocence he flaunted his favored position, seemingly unaware of how his brothers really felt about him. Suddenly uprooted from his home, Joseph immediately had to learn to cope for himself and to sort out his values and who he would be as he found his own way in adulthood.

A Journey

Typically in coming-of-age stories some sort of journey takes place or is symbolized by something. In *To Kill a Mockingbird*, the journey is to the other side of the tracks; perspective changes when looking back at home from that new vantage point. The journey in *Huckleberry Finn* takes place as Jim and Huck move down the river; the progress may be slow, but it is inevitable.

In *The Kite Runner*, the tension builds as Amir searches for Hassan. In fact, the tension has built throughout the day, beginning with breakfast, during preparation for the contest, and throughout the kite-fighting contest itself so that the moment of victory is just a pause and not the critical issue of the entire twenty-four–hour time frame. Even the kite itself can be seen as a metaphor for the journey, an attempt to flee while staying helplessly rooted in one place, a sense of detachment in a surreal world. In an indication of what is to come, Amir experiences this detachment at the moment of victory:

> I opened my eyes, saw the blue kite spinning wildly like a tire come loose from a speeding car. I blinked, tried to say something. Nothing came out. Suddenly I was hovering, looking down on myself from above. Black leather coat, red scarf, faded jeans. A thin boy, a little sallow, and a tad short for his twelve years. He had narrow shoulders and a hint of dark circles around his pale hazel eyes. The breeze rustled his light brown hair. He looked up to me and we smiled at each other. (*The Kite Runner*, 58)

Amir's journey is not complete, however, until it goes full circle. He must make the journey to America, back to Afghanistan, and back to his new life in America before he can finally believe that the events of this day are beginning to be resolved.

In *Nashville 1864*, the journey also took Steven full circle. Like Amir's, his journey was close to home, yet the experiences of Dink's death—in many ways representing the death of innocence, the death of a way of life, and the death of youthful naivete—his own physical hardships, his enlightening under-standing of the war, and his failure to find his father make his journey as great as one of many miles and greater time.

Joseph's loss-of-innocence event moved him from the security of his father's home to Egypt—a different culture, a new language, the loss of anything familiar or anything he could call his own. His journey came full circle when all of his family were reunited in this new land. Joseph does not return to the land of his people until Moses takes his bones to be buried there (Ex. 13:19), as Joseph had requested before he died (Gen. 50:25).

Responsibility and Results

In our comparison all three young men are thrust into situations they did not create, did not choose, did not instigate. Indeed, they likely could not even have imagined the events and circumstances that changed their lives.

Both *The Kite Runner* and *Nashville 1864* are so well written that the reader can easily become caught up in the events and forget that these are novels. Of the three people in our comparative stories, only Joseph is real. But his journey is the most distant in time and perhaps the most difficult for readers to identify with. If written today, it might be a *Survivor* series on television or an action-packed movie because it is full of action and plot twists, but we know little about what Joseph actually thought or felt. We do know that in a foreign land Joseph chose to live an ethical lifestyle. His circumstances show the man he really was, for he rose from slavery to governor under Pharaoh. His success could not be based on his wealth, position, or family background—except for the values instilled in him and his inherited ingenuity and ability to interpret dreams. His response to adverse circumstances was to rise above them and ultimately to forgive and restore his family.

All of the events surrounding his brief foray onto the battlefields of the American Civil War changed Steven Moore's life, but Dink's death was the most significant event in it because of Steven's role as the death occurred. Warned that the house in which they were hiding was under attack, Steven fled, thinking Dink was with him. When he discovered that Dink was not at his side, it was too late. He went back into the bombed-out building and found the slave boy's body barely visible in the rubble. He tried in vain to extricate the body, but, unable to do so, he eventually had to move on. Steven felt personally responsible for not making sure Dink got out of the house and then for not being able to give him a proper burial. His guilt for not taking care of his slave kept him from dealing with the failure of the journey to find his father, help his mother and sister, and make life better at home. The events of that winter of 1864 stayed clearly in his mind during the many years before he wrote them down. He went on to become a lawyer who entered the profession based on his own reading rather than formal education. Reading became a passion, and words enabled him to write his memoir.

Of the three young men in these stories, only Amir responded negatively. So great was his shame in what he had witnessed and his guilt for not intervening and attempting to help Hassan that he entered a downward spiral that took him years to escape. If sins can be both a result of wrongs done that should not have been done (acts of commission) and failure to do right things (acts of omission), Amir's act of omission let to sinful acts of commission. Unable to look the victim of his sin in the face, Amir sought to rid himself of his sin by creating distance. When he could not persuade his father to get rid of his servant Ali, so that his son Hassan would be gone, Amir plotted to force them to leave. By hiding his birthday money and watch in Ali's home among Hassan's possessions, he sinned himself and also made Hassan, the image of a sinless lamb, take Amir's sin on himself. And the sin he chose to ascribe to Hassan was the one his father had taught was the worse sin of all, in fact the only sin, the sin of theft. Driving Hassan and Ali away may have meant Amir no longer had to see Hassan's face, wondering if he knew that Amir had witnessed his attack. He no longer had to see the resignation in his eyes. But even with Ali and Hassan gone, the blue kite hung as a reminder of victory turned into defeat. If originally Amir had, like Hassan, been a victim rather than a perpetrator, in plotting against Hassan he moved from passive to active sinner. Then he drove that sin and guilt into silence where it lay for years—dormant in action but consuming his thoughts, self-image, and outlook on life.

A Point of No Return

Events that precipitate a loss of innocence are pivotal because the person is changed so much that nothing is ever the same. It is like looking at life through a new set of lenses; everything may be the same, but somehow everything is different. The person's worldview has changed from a childish perspective that "the world revolves around me; I am the center of the universe" to an understanding that the world is bigger than before, somehow tainted, and beyond the individual's control. In this new environment the young man must now make his way, finding out who he is and his role in the world, knowing that his power is limited and other forces will influence the shape of his life.

All our young men physically take a journey that, in one way or another, brings them full circle, but they arrive no longer boys but men. When Amir returned home with Hassan, his father greeted him with a hero's welcome:

> It happened just the way I'd imagined. I opened the door to the smoky study and stepped in. Baba and Rahim Khan were drinking tea and listening to the news crackling on the radio. Their heads turned. Then a smile played on my father's lips. He opened his arms. I put the kite down and walked into his thick hairy arms. I buried my face in the warmth of his chest and wept. Baba held me close to him, rocking me back and forth. In his arms, I forgot what I'd done. And that was good. (*The Kite Runner*, 69)

But Amir did not forget for long. He sought escape, taking advantage of his newfound favorable standing with his father to ask for time together, then not finding the experiences as fulfilling as he had hoped:

> That should have been fun, spending a day like that with Baba, hearing his stories. I finally had what I'd wanted all those years. Except now that I had it, I felt as empty as this unkempt pool I was dangling my legs into. (*The Kite Runner*, 74)

Of course, when Amir went back into Afghanistan, all of Kabul was changed under the rule of the Taliban, but even without the impact of political unrest, everything was different for Amir except the old ghosts, which remained the same:

> The house itself was far from the sprawling white mansion I remembered from my childhood. It looked smaller…The paint, once sparkling white, had faded to ghostly gray and eroded in parts, revealing the layered bricks beneath…

> I found the window to my old bedroom, second floor, third window south of the main steps to the house. I stood on tiptoes, saw nothing behind the window but shadows. Twenty-five years earlier, I had stood behind that same window, thick rain dripping down the panes and my breath fogging up the glass. I had watched Hassan and Ali load their belongings into the trunk of my father's car. (*The Kite Runner*, 229).

Coming of Age in Changing Times

Great stories, including loss-of-innocence novels, are often set in a context of local or global upheaval or societal change. Change in the world may parallel the events of the individual character's life. For example, as Huck and Jim roll down the powerful Mississippi, America is moving toward civil war and an end to a society that condones slavery. In *Nashville 1864*, not only is the life of one boy changed but also a way of living in the American South; both the gentle ways of Southern living and the evil of slavery disappeared in that decade. In *To Kill a Mockingbird*, America is again on the verge of civil unrest, the beginning of a national awareness that a minority, whether an ethnic group or those with mental and physical handicaps, will not forever remain silent and segregated. The epic story of Joseph unites a family in both place and circumstance and prepares us for their days of slavery under a pharaoh who "knew not Joseph" and the even greater epic story of Moses' leading the people out of Egypt, through the Red Sea, and on their journey to the promised land.

Likewise in *The Kite Runner*, Amir is coming of age in a country that is changing. Even before that fateful kite-fighting day, the winds of change are blowing. Afghanistan's relative calm days of monarchy have ended; and a new republic with hope and promise has arrived, but the notion of peace and prosperity will be short-lived.

First the monarchy ended:

> They weren't shooting ducks after all. As it turned out, they hadn't shot much of anything that night of July 17, 1973. Kabul awoke the next morning to find that the monarch was a thing of the past. The king, Zahir Shah, was away in Italy. In this absence, his cousin Daoud Khan had ended the king's forty-year reign with a bloodless coup. (*The Kite Runner*, 32)

And then came the republic:

> For the next couple of years, the words *economic development* and *reform* danced on a lot of lips in Kabul...For a while, a sense of rejuvenation and purpose swept across the land. People spoke of women's rights and modern technology. (*The Kite Runner*, 38)

Then came the Russian invasion that drove Baba and Amir to flee Afghanistan and take refuge in America:

> What was I doing on this road in the middle of the night? I should have been in bed, under my blanket, a book with dog-eared pages at my side. This had to be a dream. Had to be. Tomorrow morning, I'd wake up, peek out the window: No grim-faced Russian soldiers patrolling the sidewalks, no tanks rolling up and down the streets of my city, their turrets swiveling like accusing fingers, no rubble, no curfews, no Russian Army Personnel Carriers weaving through the bazaars. (*The Kite Runner*, 98)

And then the rule of the Taliban:

> That was the first time I saw the Taliban. I'd seen them on TV, on the Internet, on the cover of magazines, and in newspapers. But here I was now, less than fifty feet

from them, telling myself that the sudden taste in my mouth wasn't unadulterated, naked fear. Telling myself my flesh hadn't suddenly shrunk against my bones and my heart wasn't battering. Here they came. In all their glory. (*The Kite Runner*, 216)

Some people dislike change, fight change, seek to maintain the status quo. Others seem to embrace it. Sometimes change is thrust on people and on nations; enemies attack individuals as well as countries. And sometimes people—individuals and segments of society—will no longer tolerate oppression, slavery, or servitude, so they fight for change, the struggle coming as an internal, volcanic eruption within a person, a group, a nation. And the winds of such a change move 'round the world.

The characters in our stories find themselves in worlds that are changing. Such change causes the characters as well as the reader to see the world through different prisms, bathed in a new light. Those who cannot envision the change, like Amir, believe they will wake up the next morning and be back where they belong, in a safe world where everything is normal for them.

Not all change is good, of course, but all change can help the individual see others—perhaps for the first time. The character, and we the readers, may gain a new perspective of what it means to have a different skin color, to worship in a different way, to feel powerless or powerful, to know fear, to learn from others, and to grow as individuals.

DISCUSSION QUESTIONS

1. Do you think Hassan really dreamed about the lake and the monster or only made up the story, in the tradition the two boys had of storytelling—indeed the Afghan tradition of romantic poetry and story—to calm Amir and give him confidence for the victory ahead?

2. What caused Amir to think about vindication, salvation, and redemption before Hassan was raped? How did these concepts change after that day?

3. Does everyone have a pivotal moment, a coming-of-age event that propels them into adulthood, or is this simply a literary device?

4. How have you experienced changes in worldview as you've grown or aged? How did that change affect the way you saw home?

5. How have changing times affected your worldview and your personal life? Recall "aha" moments when you knew that you were seeing the world differently.

6. After Amir's life-changing event, he must renegotiate relationships not only with Hassan but also with his father, with Ali, with the bullies, and others. These renegotiations were the result of a negative event in his life. A new follower of Christ experiences a positive life-changing event that causes the believer to renegotiate relationships. How does a relationship with Christ help a believer with relationships? Is the negotiation of relationships as a result of either a positive or a negative life-changing experience a one-time adjustment or one that is ongoing? What evidence is there in *The Kite Runner* for your response?

For Further Reading

Jones, Madison. *Nashville 1864: The Dying of the Light*. Nashville: J. S. Sanders, 1997.

CHAPTER 2

Kites

Then I glanced up and saw a pair of kites, red with long blue tails, soaring in the sky. They danced high above the trees on the west end of the park, over the windmills.

(*The Kite Runner*, 1)

Kites are ancient and as captivating today as they ever were. Although the origins of kites are not entirely known, they apparently date back at least two to three thousand years to China.[1] They moved on, with traders' and religious leaders' help, to Korea, Japan, India, and other countries of the East, including Afghanistan, then to Europe, and eventually to North America, South America, and Australia. Each country adapted the kite to its own special design, using readily available materials and finding unique purposes for its use.

We most often think of kite flying as a children's game. A little research shows kites put to many, even surprising, uses. In Afghanistan kite flying is a competitive sport that can lead to conflict and fighting. Elsewhere types of kites have also been used extensively for scientific studies, especially about weather, and for military purposes. Who can forget the images through the years of Benjamin Franklin's scientific experiments with electricity using a kite and key while standing in the rain on a stormy night to see what would happen if lightning stuck the kite?

---

[1]Information on kites throughout this chapter came from the Web sites listed on page 104.

Kites have also had religious uses. In many cultures they continue to be used almost ritualistically. In some places, such as Afghanistan, the significance of kite flying rolls together culture, custom, tradition, and family honor in ways almost too complex to define. The people just know that it is an essential part of who they are and what they do that makes them Afghani.

The First Kites

The military, physicians, industry, and religion used early kites for varied purposes from recreation, to courtship rituals, even to committing a crime. Kites first appear in literature in a Chinese legend. A Chinese farmer tied a string to his hat to keep it from blowing away in a strong wind, and the first kite was born. Others say the first kite was invented by the Chinese general Han Hsin, who in about 200 B.C.E. during the Han Dynasty flew a kite over the walls of a city he was attacking to measure how far his army would have to tunnel to reach past the defenses. Knowing this distance, his troops reached the inside of the city, surprised their enemy, and were victorious. Another variation of this story says that the general flew thin pieces of bamboo that hummed and shrieked in the wind over the enemy camp, causing them to believe that evil spirits had come to destroy them, and so the enemy army ran away.

Another tradition claims that a Greek physician first used a kite to test his patient's eyesight. Still others claim that fishermen used the first kites in the South Sea Islands to get their bait farther out into the ocean, a practice that continues in some islands today.

In New Zealand the Maori people, believing that birds (*manu*) could carry messages between humans and gods, made their kites in the shape of birds. The Maori god Rehua is depicted as a bird, called *manu*, and was thought to be the ancestor of all kites. Kite flying was considered a sacred ritual and was often accompanied by a type of chant called the *turu manu*. The Maori also used kites for divination and for funerary purposes.

Buddhist priests from China and Korea introduced kites in Japan during the seventh century as a part of religious festivals to avert evil spirits and to ensure plentiful harvests. Kakinoki Kinsuke, a famous robber supposedly used a person-lifting kite to raise himself up to the roof of a castle adorned by statues of dolphins covered in gold scales. He stole some of the scales from the dolphins and hid them but was eventually executed for his crime.

Polynesian folklore introduces the image of the kite in a contest. In one myth, two brother gods dueled with kites. The winning brother flew his kite the highest, the continued goal of kite-flying contests there. In their mythology a kite represented the god Tane as well as the god Rongo, the patron saint of the arts, kites, and kite flying.

India claims to be the origin of the kite-flying competition that involves cutting the competition's string. Kite fliers were the sports heroes of their day and enjoyed patronage of royalty. Like competitive kite flying in Afghanistan, kite flying in India continues to be a passion, intertwining religious symbolism with competition and recreation.

Marco Polo is credited with carrying stories of kites to Europe around the end of the thirteenth century. Illustrations of the period show dragon kites on military banners. European sailors also brought kites back from Japan and Malaysia in the sixteenth and seventeenth centuries, but for many years Europeans regarded kites as little more than curiosities.

Kites in Science, Industry, and the Military

During the industrial revolution science and industry used kites in experiments. Alexander Wilson used kites to learn about wind and weather. Sir George Caley, Samuel Langley, Lawrence Hargrave, Alexander Graham Bell, Lawrence Hargrave, and the Wright Brothers experimented with kites in their efforts to develop manned flight and to use meteorological instruments and cameras.

Malaysia Airlines uses as its corporate logo a stylized moon kite intended to communicate that customers can expect from their company all the attributes associated with the best kite—elegance, performance, and attention to detail.

Interest in kiting has grown throughout the past fifty years. Gone are silk and bamboo. New materials like nylon, fiberglass, and carbon graphite have made kites stronger, lighter, more colorful, and more durable. Kite inventions and adaptations contributed to the development of modern hang gliders and sports parachutes.

In 1999, a team used kite power to pull sleds to the North Pole. Kite competitions are held in many places in North America. Some have adopted the Eastern practice of kite fighting, but most prizes are awarded for the best kite of each type, winning participants in different age groups, the highest flight, or the most artistic design.

Kites in Afghanistan

Kite flying in Afghanistan symbolizes national pride, history, fierce independence, personal pride, and religion. Traditional Afghan contests did not reward the highest flyer, the most beautiful, or the kite with the most acrobatic moves—unless those moves resulted in destroying the competition. Afghan kite flying is more aptly called kite fighting. The goal is to cut the string of all the other kites so that your kite flies alone. In the book, kite fliers may not have been aware of all that was tied up in the sport, but they were keenly aware of its importance.

> The kite-fighting tournament was an old winter tradition in Afghanistan... People gathered on sidewalks and roofs to cheer for their kids. The streets filled with kite fighters...
>
> One time, a bratty Hindi kid whose family had recently moved into the neighborhood told us that in his hometown, kite fighting had strict rules and regulations...
>
> Hassan and I looked at each other. Cracked up. The Hindi kid would soon learn what the British learned earlier in the century, and what the Russians would eventually learn by the late 1980s: that Afghans are an independent people. Afghans cherish custom but abhor rules. And so it was with kite fighting. (*The Kite Runner*, 45).

The kite fliers themselves may not have realized any religious connections except in their pleas to win:

> All I saw was the blue kite. All I smelled was victory. Salvation. Redemption. If Baba was wrong and there

was a God like they said in school, then He'd let me win…If there was a God, He'd guide the winds, let them blow for me so that, with a tug of my string, I'd cut loose my pain, my longing. I'd endured too much, come too far. And suddenly, just like that, hope became knowledge. I was going to win. It was just a matter of when. (*The Kite Runner*, 57)

For Amir, kite flying became in that moment a metaphor for life.

Kite flying was one of the first activities the Taliban outlawed, perhaps because of the ancient Buddhist symbolism related to kites or perhaps simply because almost all forms of entertainment were banned as being "un-Islamic." During their rule, kite flying became a daring act of defiance and patriotism. Getting caught meant losing your kite and being beaten. Today the skies in Kabul are once again filled with colorful kites, and kite sellers abound.

There evidently are no rules, but there are established ways of flying a kite in Afghanistan. In the book the narrator makes it clear that the construction of the kite was important.

It quickly became apparent that Hassan and I were better kite fighters than kite makers. Some flaw or other in our design always spelled its doom. So Baba started taking us to Saifo's to buy our kites. Saifo was…the city's most famous kite maker. (*The Kite Runner*, 44)

Size is not necessarily a determining factor. Kites range in size from ten to twelve inches across to as much as five or six feet long. They are usually made of thin paper and bamboo strips. The strips are not usually used in the America style of crossing the strips to make a frame for the kite. Rather they are curved around the top to give flexibility.

The string is equally important. It has to be strong to cut the opponent's string. A variety of types, materials, and thicknesses are used. Preparing the string for the contest is a time-consuming project. Glass is ground to a powder. The string is saturated in a type of paste made of rice and then rolled in the powdered glass. Then it has to dry, often by wrapping it around two trees, before it is carefully rolled on a drum in preparation for the contest.

Cuts are frequent both in preparing the string and in flying the kite. Some fliers cover their index finger with a piece of leather to reduce injury. The drum has to be constructed so that it can be easily managed and can quickly release the string.

All of the equipment means nothing without the skill of the kite fliers. Two people are needed to manage both the drum and the kite. And the winner generally has a unique blend of good equipment, experience, skill, patience, and luck.

Kite running is also part of the sport. Once the string is cut and the kite soars away, the kite is up for grabs. The one who finds it has also won a contest by getting to the kite first; and he has a trophy or a kite to fly another day.

DISCUSSION QUESTIONS

1. In what ways is a kite a metaphor for Amir's life?

2. How does kite fighting characterize the experience of Afghanistan and its people?

3. In kite fighting in Afghanistan the people were said to "cherish custom but abhor rules." Was this true of other aspects of their lives or just kite fighting? Is it true of your people as well? If so, in what ways?

CHAPTER 3

Afghanistan

*People went to work Saturday through Thursday and gathered
for picnics on Fridays in parks, on the banks of Ghargha Lake,
in the gardens of Paghman. Multicolored buses and lorries
filled with passengers rolled through the narrow streets of
Kabul...On Eid, the three days of celebration after the holy
month of Ramadan, Kabulis dressed in their best and newest
clothes and visited their families...Children opened gifts and
played with dyed hard-boiled eggs.*

(*The Kite Runner,* 38)

Images of bombed-out buildings and barren landscapes of
dirt and rock, void of any living vegetation except a few straggly
bushes, are all most people today know of Afghanistan.
Television clips of this war-ravaged country leave little room
for the picture Amir draws of his homeland in the early pages
of *The Kite Runner.* His picture derives from the time before the
ongoing political upheaval that began with overthrowing the
monarchy in 1973. Most Americans know nothing of Afghanistan before Osama bin Laden, who seems in many ways to be
an appropriate symbol of Afghanistan's tragic past. It is a nation
ravaged by war throughout its history and one of the most
impoverished nations on earth.

With a population of 29,928,987, Afghanistan faces unem-
ployment of 40 percent with 53 percent of the people living
below the poverty line. The country can list an array of natural
resources—natural gas, petroleum, coal, copper, talc, sulfur, lead,

zinc, iron ore, salt, and precious and semiprecious stones—and agricultural products—opium, wheat, fruits, nuts, wool, mutton, sheepskins, and lambskins. Industry is small and includes production of textiles, soap, furniture, shoes, fertilizer, cement, hand-woven carpets, natural gas, coal, and copper. Much of the country—the mountainous regions—is unfit for agriculture. The fertile river basins and the plains form only about 12 percent of the land, so the dry land with climate extremes in summer and winter forestalls the people from producing the fruits and vegetables and other foodstuffs they love.

Still, the Afghans take pride in a rich five thousand-year-old history and culture featuring a love of poetry, competition, loyalty, courage, hospitality, kinship, love for friends, chastity, morality, respecting rights, and a determination to protect and avenge themselves and their women. The traditional meals feature beef, mutton, chicken, and turkey, but no pork for religious reasons. Shish kebabs and pilau—chicken and rice covered in a sauce of brown sugar, raisins, orange peel, carrots, and almonds—with corn roasted in the shucks and a flat, thin whole wheat bread called nan also play a large part in their diets. Having few sweets, they load up their tea with sugar and snack on almonds and walnuts baked with salt and butter.

Traditional clothing has become a battleground in Islamic Afghanistan. Before the Taliban intruded into the government, women had gained freedom from wearing the traditional chaderis to cover their faces. Men and youth had begun to adopt Western dress to a great extent, but the Taliban forced traditional Islamic dress on the people. This featured turbans nine to ten feet long, men's blousy pants a yard wide, shirts reaching to the knees or ankles, and for the well-to-do, karakui or Persian lamb caps.

A Tribal Society: Pashtuns and Hazara

Afghanistan is a traditional Asian tribal society. Each of the ethnic groups in Afghanistan has its own cultural traits based on language and custom. However, they share certain things in common. Tribes are traditionally patriarchal in a system that is reinforced by Islam, the religion of all Afghan tribal groups.

The Pashtuns make up half the population. Almost all (99 percent) are Sunni Muslims. They have distinctive customs and traditions and an unwritten code of ethics called *Pashtunwali* ("the way of the Pashtun"), which is followed religiously. It includes *melmastia* (hospitality and protection to guests), *badal* (the right of blood feuds or revenge), *tureh* (bravery), and *purdah* (protection of women).

Fewer than .01 percent of Pashtuns are Christians. There is no visible Pashtun church, although a number of believers meet in small groups in some areas. Most Pashtuns have no access to the gospel in any form. Radio broadcasts are available, but there is little opportunity to promote the broadcasts. There is no scripture in the Southern Pashto language. Except in a few locations, there is no known Christian witness. Because of severe persecution, most Pashtun believers remain secret most of their lives out of fear that they will lose their families, jobs, opportunities in their society, and even their lives. The trial in 2006 of an Afghan man charged with converting to Christianity (punishable by death) brought to world attention this persecution.

The minority Hazaras have been less fortunate than the Pashtuns. In the later part of the nineteenth century, the Hazara tribal system was destroyed. Hazaras' personal property and land were taken, as they were made slaves and sold in the Kabul bazaar. Many Hazaras fled to Pakistan and Iran. In the early part of the twentieth century, slavery, with some exceptions, was outlawed; however, those already in slavery were not freed. A decade later Shah Amanullah (1919–1929) outlawed slavery and returned seized land and property to the Hazaras.

But the old practices of subjugation of Hazaras continued. While not technically slaves, they were not treated much better, earning low pay as servants laboring as attendants, cooks, housekeepers, drivers, midwives, clothes washers, and yard workers in many middle-class to high-ranking households.

The extended family is the important social and economic unit in Afghanistan. The eldest male, usually the grandfather, controls the family money and makes all decisions regarding the family's activities and welfare. The eldest female, usually his wife, runs the household and is in charge of the other women, including her daughters, the wives of her sons, any other wives her husband may have (Islam allows each man to have four wives, but most Afghan men are too poor to afford them), and any unmarried or widowed cousins or aunts who live with the family. While hospitable to guests, Afghans are intensely private and resent any outside interference in their homes.

Afghans are known for their constant sense of competition, whether among tribal families for land, work, and food or in the legendary toughness and resilience of the Afghan fighter. Afghan legend, poetry, and myth are full of stories of war, victory against incredible odds, and heroic individual struggles. The competitive nature is seen in kite fighting as well as in the favorite sport of Afghanistan, *buzkashi,* in which a player riding a horse tries to take a calf carcass (or goat carcass) down the field and pitch it across the goal line.

Love of poetry marks the Afghan people. The idealized Afghan leader is both warrior and poet, and poetry is the chief literary form of most Afghanis. Poetry is recited at almost every social occasion and at political or tribal gatherings. Many of the most famous poets were illiterate as this is a verbal, not a written, culture. Some, however, did write down their own poetry.

The control by the oldest male (patriarchal control), intense family loyalty, insistence on privacy, love of poetry, and toughness are all evident in *The Kite Runner.*

History[1]

Recent warfare is nothing new to Afghanistan history. Its landlocked people have had to defend their nation and its freedom, as people fought over the all-important and famous thirty-three-mile Khyber Pass through the Hindu Kush mountain range on the Pakistan-Afghanistan border. Today Pakistan controls the pass, but many others have occupied it through history. Neighbors from the adjacent countries of China, Pakistan, Tajikistan, Uzbekistan, Turkmenistan, and Iran have intruded on Afghanistan's property. So have Greek, Persian,

---

[1]Information in this chapter is shaped by Adam Ritscher, "A Brief History of Afghanistan," www.afghangovernment.com/briefhistory.htm. Other important sources are listed on page 104.

Mongol, Tartar, Indian, and British soldiers. Recent intruders include Russia and the United States. Such intrusions result from various motives—land and power lust, trade and economic issues, religious conversion, and transportation needs.

For hundreds of years, great camel caravans traveled through the Khyber Pass, bringing silks and porcelain from China to trade in the Middle East. Often they stopped at Herat, the great oasis in western Afghanistan. Armies since those of Alexander the Great have also passed through this gap in the mountains. The British constructed a road through the pass in 1879 and converted it into a highway during the 1920s. A railroad was also built through the pass in the 1920s. Today the railroad and two highways move through the pass, one for cars and trucks and the other for traditional camel caravans.

The capital city of Afghanistan is Kabul, at about six thousand feet elevation in the heart of one of the most fertile parts of the country. Among at least a dozen ethnic groups, Pashtuns have in many ways controlled the country, forming approximately half the population and providing its royal family. The next largest group is the Takiks. Hazaras, a Mongol people claiming descent from Genghis Khan, are one of the smaller groups.

During the eighth and ninth centuries Arabs brought Islam to Afghanistan and ruled the country. Islam became the dominant religion—80 percent Sunni and 19 percent Shi'a. Small numbers of Hindu, Sikhs, and Jews also live there. When Arab rule began to break down, semi-independent states began to form, but the Mongols crushed them during the thirteenth century and controlled the land until the sixteenth century when Afghanistan was caught between the Mughals of northern India and the Safavids of Iran. Armies from both sides devastated the country.

In 1747 Ahmed Shah, a Pashtun, replaced a deceased Iranian ruler, beginning a 200-year run of home rule; but even this was marked by revolt and civil wars. Then Russia and Britain became involved in the 1800s, and the country had to deal once again with imperialist forces. The British controlled India and looked toward Afghanistan with its mountains as a desirable natural land barrier. Expanding to the south and controlling more and more of central Asia, the Russians also set their sights on the Afghan mountains. Finally, Afghanistan regained independence in 1919 but suffered under strong dictatorships who did not care about the people's welfare.

In 1973 a republic was declared, but the change was apparently in name only. The new ruler, Daoud, simply called himself president instead of king. An underground communist party with ties to Moscow—called the Peoples' Democratic Party of Afghanistan (PDPA)—assisted Daoud in seizing power. When Daoud had established power, he took steps to get rid of the PDPA. But his plan failed, and in 1978 they took power from Daoud in a military coup. They declared Afghanistan a secular state and began instituting limited reforms, such as declaring women equal to men. They tried to end the practice of purchasing brides and attempted a land reform program. These reforms met stiff opposition from religious groups, leading to open rebellion in rural areas. Infighting resulted between conservative and liberal factions within the party.

The Soviet Union invaded in the midst of the confusion and took power in 1979, making Karmal, the leader of the moderate faction of the PDPA, the new head of state. A third of all Afghanis fled the country during this ten-year occupation. Pakistan and Iran gave shelter to more than six million refugees. Islamic fundamentalists, assisted by the United States, continued to oppose the government during this time. They operated from camps set up by the CIA, who provided training and billions of dollars of sophisticated weaponry for these Mujahideen, meaning "holy warriors." Arabs joined them in a call to "holy war" against the Soviet Union. One young man, a Saudi, became a popular CIA operative in its war on communism; his name was Osama bin Laden.

Tired of the expense of trying to keep control, the Soviets withdrew in 1989. With the Soviet threat gone, the CIA also lost interest, leaving the battle once again to the PDPA and the Mujahideen. In 1992 the Mujahideen finally secured control.

Various warlords took control of the different regions of the country, and some regained control in the 2001 war that ousted the Taliban. Northern Alliance leader Burhanuddin Rabbani, who took Kabul from the Taliban in 2001, had previously ruled over the city from 1992 until 1996. Under his control more than sixty thousand people were murdered, and thousands of women were raped. Rashid Dostun is now in control of the city of Mazar-E-Sharif, where he also ruled from 1992 until 1997. Likewise Ismail Khan ruled the city of Heart from 1992 to 1995 and is again in control of that region, and Yunis Khalis is again in control of Jalabad, which he ruled previously from 1992 to 1996. The factions of the PDPA continued to fight in the early 1990s, leaving the country in an ongoing state of civil war.

Although the CIA lost interest in the 1990s, the Pakistani government did not. Their intelligence forces aided in establishing the Taliban, a new Islamic fundamentalist movement. Leaders were mostly Pashtuns, young and religious. They came with a zeal to restore order and Islam. Many in the war-weary population at first welcomed the new movement, hoping for a return to peace and normalcy. The city-ruling warlords didn't relinquish their territory easily, however. They eventually united and continued to fight as the Northern Alliance. However, by mid-2001 their control was diminished to approximately 10 percent of the country.

The Taliban sought to institute a theocratic government based on their conservative interpretation of the Koran. Women were forced to wear veils and prohibited from attending school or holding jobs outside the home. Television, kite flying, and other forms of entertainment were banned. Afghanistan, more and more repressed, was becoming politically and diplomatically isolated.

Then came September 11, 2001. The U.S. government demanded that the Taliban hand over Osama bin Laden, which, of course, the Taliban refused to do. The U.S. bombing of Afghanistan provided impetus to the old warlords, who eventually regained power over their previously held cities. With help from the United States and the United Nations, in January 2004 Afghanistan adopted its new constitution, establishing the country as an Islamic Republic.

Today, after decades of war, the economy is still in ruins, and the environment is in a state of crisis. Presidential elections were held on October 9, 2004, with more than a million Afghans voting. The Joint Electoral Management Body of Afghanistan certified the elections on November 3, and declared Hamid Karzai, the interim president, the winner with 55.4 percent of the votes.

DISCUSSION QUESTIONS

1. How is the history of Afghanistan evident in Amir's early years, before his twelfth birthday?

2. The people of Afghanistan are tough, independent, private, and poetry lovers. How are these characteristics evident in the people in Afghanistan? Do they change when they come to America? If so, how?

3. How is Islam a characteristic of Afghanistan?

CHAPTER 4

Fathers and Sons, Brothers and Friends

Baba would buy us each three identical kites and spools of glass string. If I changed my mind and asked for a bigger and fancier kite, Baba would buy it for me—but then he'd buy it for Hassan too. Sometimes I wished he wouldn't do that. Wished he'd let me be the favorite.

(*The Kite Runner*, 44–45)

The drama of biblical stories is found in other ancient writings, but the writings of the Bible are more familiar to us. Similar themes occur in other writings: tales of trickery, sibling rivalry and even fratricide, conflict between fathers and sons, plotting mothers, jealousy among women, miscommunication and lack of understanding, and the ongoing cycle of life. But we are "People of the Book"—the phrase used by Muhammad when referring to Muslims, Christians, and Jews and their common reverence for the revealed word of God—and so we delve into these sacred texts not only to learn about God but to learn more about ourselves. The themes are ageless, and we find many of them once again in the pages of *The Kite Runner*. This is especially true of the stories of the patriarchs.

Muslims hold much in common with Jews and Christians in their reverence for the Genesis stories. And, after all, the story of the patriarchs is about the relationships of fathers and sons, and of brothers. A brief look at the patriarchs, as portrayed in the Old Testament or Hebrew Scriptures, can serve as preparation to look at *The Kite Runner* in light of these ancient stories.

Abraham is the first of the patriarchs. God promised him that his progeny would be more numerous than the stars in the sky or the grains of sand in the desert. He would be the father not only of many children but also of many nations. God summoned Abram (later called Abraham) to leave his home without knowing where he was going, and in faith Abram obeyed. But the years went by, and Abram remained childless. Periodically God renewed his covenant with Abram. At last, when Abram was getting old and still without a son or daughter, his wife Sarai (later called Sarah), decided that something must be done. So she sent her maid Hagar to Abram, and Hagar became pregnant by him. But after it became clear that Hagar was with child, Sarah became jealous and treated Hagar so cruelly that she ran away. However, in a vision God told Hagar to return home and have the baby. Abram was eighty-six when Ishmael was born.

When Abraham (God changed his name at age 99) was one hundred years old, Isaac was born to him and Sarah. Sarah demanded that Abraham send away Hagar and Ishmael. Though it saddened him, Abraham sent them away because God assured him that though Isaac was the child of promise, Ishmael would also father a nation. Abraham had additional sons with other wives and concubines, but, the Bible says, he left all he had to Isaac. Nonetheless, Ishmael reappeared when Abraham died, and Isaac and Ishmael buried their father together.

One notable event in the life of Abraham and Isaac is the call of God for Abraham once again to renew his covenant with God through sacrifice, the sacrifice of his beloved son Isaac. In faith Abraham took Isaac to the place of sacrifice. As they prepared the wood for the fire, Isaac asked his father where the animal was for the sacrifice. Abraham responded that the Lord would provide the sacrifice. Just as Abraham was about to kill his son, God provided a lamb to die in Isaac's place.

As noted, this is the story from the Hebrew Bible. In the Muslim tradition Ishmael was the child of promise and

Abraham's heir. Abraham took Ishmael, not Isaac, to be sacrificed. Like Jacob a generation later, Ishmael had twelve sons who formed twelve tribes. And today the descendants of Ishmael outnumber those of Isaac.

Isaac had two sons. Jacob and Esau were twins; Esau was born first. And whether born first by minutes or by years, being born first meant that Esau would, according to law, receive the birthright from his father. The elder son of a family received a double portion of the family inheritance. The birthright also generally included becoming the leader of the family after the death of the father.

Through an act of cunning, Jacob got the birthright from Esau. Esau was his father's favorite, but Jacob was his mother's favorite. Esau was a hunter, ruddy, an outdoorsmen, while Jacob stayed close to home. When Esau was out hunting, Jacob prepared a lentil stew. When Esau came in from the hunt, he was hungry and asked Jacob for some stew. Jacob responded that he would give Esau the stew in exchange for his birthright.

Jacob's name suggests his cunning nature. The word was the same as that used for the serpent in the Genesis story of the fall. The serpent would bruise the heel (deceive) humankind. The Bible records this story of the twins' birth: "When her time to give birth was at hand, there were twins in her womb. The first came out red, all his body like a hairy mantle; so they named him Esau. Afterward his brother came out, with his hand gripping Esau's heel; so he was named Jacob" (Gen. 25:24–26). Grabbing at someone's heel suggests more than a birth position; it often means someone who deceives others, someone who is subtle and conniving. And so it was with Jacob. His plan to rob Esau of his birthright set the stage for the kind of person he would become and was the first of many acts of deception.

Apparently the two sons continued to live together, however, as long as Isaac remained head of the household. But as Isaac neared death, he wanted to bless his favorite, Esau. But first he asked Esau to go hunt some game and prepare it for Isaac to eat. Rebekah, the boys' mother, overheard this conversation and repeated it to Jacob. Together, mother and son plotted to steal Isaac's blessing for Esau.

While Esau was out hunting, Jacob killed two sheep, and Rebekah prepared them to taste like wild game. And because Esau was hairy and Jacob was fair, Rebekah used the skins to make arm coverings for Jacob, and she dressed Jacob in Esau's best clothing, appropriate for such an occasion.

Jacob, showing both his cunning and his cowardice, feared Isaac would know he was not Esau and would curse rather than bless him. To which Rebekah replied, "Let your curse be on me, my son" (Gen. 27:13).

So Jacob went in to the nearly blind Isaac. Isaac was apparently suspicious, for he asked Jacob, "Who are you, my son?" (Gen. 27:18), and, "How is it that you have found it [the game] so quickly, my son?" (v. 20). And then, as Jacob had anticipated, Isaac requested, "Come near, that I may feel you, my son, to know whether you are really my son Esau or not" (v. 21). Still, after feeling the hair on Jacob's hands, Isaac was not convinced, "Are you really my son Esau?" (v. 24). But Isaac ate and then told Jacob to come near for the blessing. Again he showed his suspicion by feeling his clothing and smelling him. And then he blessed Jacob.

Immediately after this Esau returned home and began to prepare the game for his father, as instructed. But he quickly learned that Jacob had already received the blessing intended for him. Fathers could give all their children a blessing, but he had planned a special blessing for Esau, his favorite son. That blessing, which Jacob received, was:

"May God give you of the dew of heaven,
and of the fatness of the earth,
and plenty of grain and wine.
Let peoples serve you,
and nations bow down to you.
Be lord over your brothers,
and may your mother's sons bow down to you.
Cursed be everyone who curses you,
and blessed be everyone who blesses you!"

(Gen. 27:28–29)

Now Isaac had only the blessing he'd intended for Jacob, and so he gave it to Esau:

"See, away from the fatness of the earth shall your home be,
  and away from the dew of heaven on high.
By your sword you shall live,
  and you shall serve your brother;
but when you break loose,
  you shall break his yoke from your neck."

(Gen. 27:39–40)

This "blessing" sounds almost like a curse.

Esau wept and hated Jacob and vowed that after his father died he would kill his brother. When Rebekah heard about this, she called Jacob in and, fearing for his life, told him to prepare to leave to go to Haran to live with his uncle Laban. Rebekah told Isaac that she could not bear to lose both her husband and her son, so he agreed with her to send Jacob to Haran. But before Jacob left, Isaac gave him further instructions. And again he blessed him, "May God Almighty bless you and make you fruitful and numerous, that you may become a company of peoples. May he give to you the blessing of Abraham, to you and to your offspring with you, so that you may take possession of the land where you now live as an alien—land that God gave to Abraham" (Gen. 28:3–4).

Jacob left home; and on his journey to Haran, he had a dream. It's the first dream recorded in the Bible. With a stone for his pillow, he lay down under the stars and dreamed of a ladder reaching up into heaven. And in that dream he saw at the top of the ladder God, who delivered yet another blessing:

"I am the LORD, the God of Abraham your father and the God of Isaac; the land on which you lie I will give to you and to your offspring; and your offspring shall be like the dust of the earth, and you shall spread abroad to the west and to the east and to the north and to the south; and all the families of the earth shall be blessed in you and in your offspring. Know that I am with you and will keep you wherever you go, and will bring you back to this land; for I will not leave you until I have done what I have promised you." (Gen. 28:13–16)

In Haran, Jacob continued to live up to his name as a trickster. But his uncle Laban was also a deceiver, and, living together, they plotted against each other. Laban tricked Jacob into working for fourteen years instead of seven for his wife Rachel. And each tried to deceive the other in separating their herds of sheep and goats. Eventually the tension grew, and Jacob decided to leave Laban, taking his family and herds with him. Jacob left when Laban was away from his tents, out shearing the sheep. Jacob had been gone for three days before Laban, who had been out with the sheep, discovered he was gone. And, though Jacob apparently didn't know it, Rachel had taken Laban's household gods.

Laban caught up with Jacob and asked him why he had taken his family and herds and left. Jacob denied having the household gods and said the one who had stolen them would be killed. Laban searched for the household gods but did not find them because Rachel had hidden them by sitting on them. Laban and Jacob parted peacefully, and Jacob turned toward home so that he could also make peace with his brother Esau.

Jacob sent messengers ahead of him to Esau. The servants returned, reporting to Jacob that Esau was on his way to meet him with four hundred men, and Jacob was afraid. So Jacob divided his people and his flocks and herds so that if Esau took one group the rest might have a chance of escape.

Jacob took a gift of goats, sheep, camels, cows, and donkeys and sent his servant to take them to Esau as a peace offering. He hoped that once the two saw each other Esau would accept him.

After praying for deliverance, Jacob sent his family away and lay down to sleep alone. A man appeared and wrestled with Jacob until daybreak. He did not tell Jacob his name, but the man blessed Jacob and changed his name to Israel. And Jacob said, "I have seen God face to face, and yet my life is preserved" (Gen. 32:30).

Jacob looked up and saw Esau approaching, but Jacob need not have been afraid, for Esau ran to him and embraced him. Their relationship was restored.

Jacob had received the blessing and the birthright. He had twelve sons who formed the twelve tribes of Israel four hundred years later when Moses led the Israelites out of Egyptian slavery.

Esau also had many sons; his descendants were called the Edomites.

One of Jacob's sons was Joseph, whose story is recounted in chapter 6 of this book.

Fathers and Sons

The biblical stories of fathers and sons are not limited to the patriarchs, of course. We could also look at the stories of Adam and the relationship of his sons Cain and Abel, a sibling rivalry that ends with the firstborn killing the favored second born. We've already looked at Jacob's sons, what happened when they could not get along, and the rise to power of Joseph, a favored younger son. David, another younger son, had sons who fought with one another and even against their own father.

The patriarchs, however, contain examples enough for our comparison with *The Kite Runner*. The generations of the patriarchs tell the stories of three fathers—Abraham, Isaac, and Jacob. All three had sons—favorite sons and other sons. All three families had conflict because of the sons. Let's take a closer look.

Sons Take on the Traits of Their Fathers

Abraham was a man of faith. Though it seems somewhat less apparent in his son and grandson, they, too, were men who worshiped and obeyed God. Men of the covenant, they inherited their father's promise from God to inherit the land and populate it and to bless all the earth.

Jacob was a deceiver who betrayed his brother, and ten of his sons apparently followed in the "family tradition." They sold their brother Joseph into slavery and deceived their father so that he would think Joseph had been killed by wild animals.

Joseph, like his father, was a dreamer and an interpreter of dreams. God spoke to Jacob through dreams, and God gave Joseph the gift to interpret dreams, which paved his escape from prison and his rise to power.

Amir also learned from his father. Baba's doubts about religion fed Amir's young questioning mind. When Baba told Amir that the only sin was theft, that was the sin Amir chose to try to force Hassan and Ali to leave in disgrace. Ultimately, of course, theft and deceit were traits father and son had in common. Both had betrayed the friends who loved them most. Baba betrayed Ali, and Amir betrayed Hassan.

Baba could be cruel and distant, and Amir also displayed these traits from time to time. And Baba could be generous and take risks on behalf of another, even at the risk of losing his own life. This was another lesson Amir learned and put into practice.

Both father and son could also be completely selfless, even to the point of risking their life for others. Baba risked his life to save a woman he didn't know from an aggressive Russian guard. Baba built an orphanage; Amir risked his life to adopt an orphan.

When Baba and Amir came to America, they depended on each other more and more. When Amir and Soraya married, they lived with Baba, and Amir could hardly imagine life without him. At Baba's funeral, responding to visitors who came to pay respect to Baba, Amir realized the change that was about to occur in his life:

> Listening to them, I realized how much of who I was, what I was, had been defined by Baba and the marks he had left on people's lives. My whole life, I had been "Baba's son." Now he was gone. Baba couldn't show me the way anymore; I'd have to find it on my own. (*The Kite Runner,* 152)

Fathers Love Their Sons

Every man in the biblical stories wanted a son, someone to carry on the family name and lineage. When God called Abraham and promised to make a great nation of him, he promised him a son. "Then the word of the LORD came to him: 'This man will not be your heir, but a son coming from your own body will be your heir'" (Gen. 15:4, NIV). The sons' names are those most often listed in the biblical "begats." Having sons was very important in that culture, as it is in many parts of the world today.

Abraham loved both his sons. After Isaac was born, Sarah told Abraham to send Hagar and Ishmael away. He eventually did this because God assured him that Isaac would carry his lineage, but "the matter was very distressing to Abraham on account of his son [Ishmael]" (Gen. 21:11). He also loved Isaac: "The child [Isaac] grew, and was weaned; and Abraham made a great feast on the day that Isaac was weaned" (Gen. 21:8). And when God told Abraham to sacrifice Isaac, he said: "Abraham!...Take your son, your only son Isaac, whom you love, and go to the land of Moriah, and offer him there as a burnt offering on one of the mountains that I shall show you" (Gen. 22:1–2).

Isaac also wanted sons: "Isaac prayed to the LORD for his wife, because she was barren" (Gen. 25:21). And he loved his sons, Jacob and Esau—he just loved Esau a little bit more: "When the boys grew up, Esau was a skillful hunter, a man of the field, while Jacob was a quiet man, living in tents. Isaac loved Esau, because he was fond of game; but Rebekah loved Jacob" (Gen. 25:27). Isaac also loved Jacob and blessed him—not just the blessing intended for Esau that Jacob stole, but a blessing for him as he sent him out to find a non-Canaanite wife:

> "May God almighty bless you and make you fruitful and numerous, that you may become a company of peoples. May he give to you the blessing of Abraham, to you and to your offspring with you, so that you may take possession of the land where you now live as an alien—land that God gave to Abraham." (Gen. 28:3–4)

Jacob also loved his sons, especially Joseph, and his partiality showed: "When his brothers saw that their father loved him [Joseph] more than all his brothers, they hated him, and could not speak peaceably to him" (Gen. 37:4).

And in *The Kite Runner,* fathers loved their sons, but both Ali and Baba had been deprived of their fathers when they were very young. "Ali, who had been orphaned at the age of five, had no worldly possessions or inheritance to speak of" (*The Kite Runner,* 9). And, "When Baba was six, a thief walked into my grandfather's house in the middle of the night. My grandfather, a respected judge, confronted him, but the thief stabbed him in the throat, killing him instantly—and robbing Baba of a father" (*The Kite Runner,* 16).

Ali loved Hassan, and Baba loved both Amir and Hassan. Of course, at the beginning of the book, we don't know that Baba is actually Hassan's father. Ali knew, but he loved Hassan intensely, the son he would raise, knowing he'd likely never have a son of his own. "Ali was immune to the insults of his assailants; he had found his joy, his antidote, the moment Sanaubar had given birth to Hassan" (*The Kite Runner,* 9). He showed concern for Hassan after the rape, knowing that something had happened but not knowing what, and he questioned Amir about it, only to be rebuffed. And later when Ali and Hassan left Kabul because Amir had made Hassan look like a thief: "Ali drew Hassan to him, curled his arm around his son's shoulder. It was a protective gesture and I knew whom Ali was protecting him from" (*The Kite Runner,* 92).

And Baba loved Hassan. Like Abraham and Isaac, sometimes it appeared that he loved his second son even more than he loved his first. Amir knew that Baba loved Hassan. Baba gave Hassan extravagant gifts for his birthday, one year giving him surgery to correct his harelip. Amir knew it was a gift of love: "I wished I too had some kind of scar that would beget Baba's sympathy. It wasn't fair. Hassan hadn't done anything to earn Baba's affections; he'd just been born with that stupid harelip" (*The Kite Runner,* 40).

And when Hassan falsely confessed to stealing Amir's watch and money, Baba was quick to say, "I forgive you" (*The Kite Runner,* 92). Even for the sin of stealing, a father can forgive the son he loves.

Amir may not have realized just how much his father loved him until they were in America:

> For me, America was a place to bury my memories.
>
> For Baba, a place to mourn his.
>
> "Maybe we should go back to Peshawar," I said...
>
> "You were happier there, Baba. It was more like home," I said.
>
> "Peshawar was good for me. Not good for you."
>
> "You work so hard here."
>
> "It's not so bad now," he said, meaning since he had become the day manager at the gas station. But I'd seen the way he winced and rubbed his wrists on damp days.

The way sweat erupted on his forehead as he reached for his bottle of antacids after meals. "Besides, I didn't bring us here for me, did I?"

I reached across the table and put my hand on his. My student hand, clean and soft, on his laborer's hand, grubby and calloused. I thought of all the trucks, train sets, and bikes he'd bought me in Kabul. Now America. One last gift for Amir. (*The Kite Runner,* 113)

And later when Amir graduated from high school:

That summer of 1983, I graduated from high school at the age of twenty, by far the oldest senior tossing his mortarboard on the football field that day. I remember losing Baba in the swarm of families, flashing cameras, and blue gowns...Then he saw me and waved. Smiled. He motioned for me to wear my mortarboard, and took a picture of me with the school's clock tower in the background. I smiled for him—in a way, this was his day more than mine. He walked to me, curled his arm around my neck, and gave my brow a single kiss. "I am *moftakhir,* Amir," he said. Proud. His eyes gleamed when he said that and I liked being on the receiving end of that look. (*The Kite Runner,* 114)

Even on this special day, after giving Amir the car he'd work so hard to get for him, Baba said, thinking of the second son he loved so much, "I wish Hassan had been with us today" (*The Kite Runner,* 116).

Sons Want to Please Their Fathers

When Abraham took Isaac to sacrifice him, there is no indication that Isaac resisted in any way. He was obedient and wanted to please his father.

When Jacob was seeking to steal Esau's birthright from his father, he dressed appropriately and sought to please his father with the food he'd requested. Yes, it was a manipulative act of trickery; but in some ways it was still a desperate attempt to please his father. Later, when his father sent him away to Laban, Jacob obeyed his father and did not marry a Canaanite woman, as his father had instructed him. Obedience, as with Isaac and

Jacob, is one way sons have of showing respect and trying to please their fathers.

Joseph also sought to please Jacob. He obediently went to check on his brothers, obeying his father. Then much later in Egypt, Jacob longed to see his father again. Perhaps part of the reason he was so gracious to his brothers was to please his father.

Hassan just seemed to please both Ali and Baba. He didn't seem to have to do much to get their approval. Perhaps that's as it should be but clearly isn't always the case. As a boy Amir couldn't do anything to please his father. Part of Amir's feeling that his father didn't love him may have been a result of his own guilt for the death of his mother:

> I always felt like Baba hated me a little. And why not? After all, I *had* killed his beloved wife, his beautiful princess, hadn't I? The least I could have done was to have had the decency to have turned out a little more like him. But I hadn't turned out like him. Not at all. (*The Kite Runner*, 17)

Then, after Amir cried when he saw a man trampled to death at a *buzkashi* tournament, he overheard a conversation between his father and Rahim Kahn:

> "He's always buried in those books or shuffling around the house like he's lost in some dream."…
>
> "I wasn't like that." Baba sounded frustrated, almost angry.
>
> Rahim Khan laughed. "Children aren't coloring books. You don't get to fill them with your favorite colors."
>
> "I'm telling you," Baba said, "I wasn't like that at all, and neither were any of the kids I grew up with."…
>
> "There is something missing in that boy."…
>
> "You just need to let him find his way," Rahim Khan said."…
>
> "If I hadn't see the doctor pull him out of my wife with my own eyes, I'd never believe he's my son." (*The Kite Runner*, 19–20)

That's why the kite-fighting contest was so important. It was finally a chance to please his father. And for a time, at least, it did just that.

Sons Want Their Fathers' Blessing

For "People of the Book," blessing begins in Genesis. God first blessed the birds and the fish in Genesis 1:

> So God created the great sea monsters and every living creature that moves, of every kind, with which the waters swarm, and every winged bird of every kind. And God saw that it was good. God blessed them, saying, "Be fruitful and multiply and fill the waters in the seas, and let birds multiply on the earth." (vv. 21–22)

Then he blessed humankind with a similar command:

> God blessed them, and God said to them, "Be fruitful and multiply, and fill the earth and subdue it; and have dominion over the fish of the sea and over the birds of the air and over every living thing that moves upon the earth." (Gen. 1:28)

God also blessed the seventh day of the week (Gen. 2:3). Noah is the first person specifically mentioned in the Bible calling on God to bless others: "Blessed by the LORD my God be Shem" (Gen. 9:26). But Abraham is the first person in the Bible whom God said would bless others:

> Now the LORD said to Abram, "Go from your country and our kindred and your father's house to the land that I will show you. I will make of you a great nation, and I will bless you, and make your name great, so that you will be a blessing. I will bless those who bless you, and the one who curses you I will curse; and in you all the families of the earth shall be blessed." (Gen. 12:1–3)

In Genesis 17, after learning from God that Ishmael was not the son of the promise, Abraham asked God to bless Ishmael, and God answered, "As for Ishmael, I have heard you; I will bless him and make him fruitful and exceedingly numerous;

he shall be the father of twelve princes, and I will make him a great nation" (v. 20).

But the blessings of Isaac for Jacob and Esau are the ones that are memorable for most people. Esau was willing to sell his birthright, his extra portion of material goods and the role as head of the family, for a bowl of lentil stew. But he had to be tricked out of his father's blessing. "Now Esau hated Jacob because of the blessing with which his father had blessed him, and Esau said to himself, 'The days of mourning for my father are approaching; then I will kill my brother Jacob'" (27:41). Such was and is the importance of a father's blessing.

Baba had a unique way of blessing Amir. Shortly before Baba's death, Amir came in to find his wife Soraya at his father's side:

> One day, I came home from the pharmacy with Baba's morphine pills. Just as I shut the door, I caught a glimpse of Soraya quickly sliding something under Baba's blanket. "Hey, I saw that! What were you two doing?" I said.
>
> "Nothing," Soraya said, smiling.
>
> "Liar." I lifted Baba's blanket. "What's this?" I said, though as soon as I picked up the leather-bound book, I knew. I traced my fingers along the gold-stitched borders. I remembered the fireworks the night Rahim Khan had given it to me, the night of my thirteenth birthday, flares sizzling and exploding into bouquets of red, green, and yellow.
>
> "I can't believe you can write like this," Soraya said.
>
> Baba dragged his head off the pillow. "I put her up to it. I hope you don't mind."
>
> I gave the notebook back to Soraya and left the room. Baba hated it when I cried. (*The Kite Runner,* 150–51)

Even today the blessing of the father on a son is of paramount importance. In the January 2006 issue of *Christianity Today,* former NFL player Bill Glass tells about a book he has written with Terry Pluto, *Champions for Life: The Healing Power of a Father's Blessing* (Faith Communications, 2005). The book is based on his thirty-six years of prison ministry. In the article he says that the biggest problem in America today is the lack of fathers' blessings on their sons.

Glass recalls:

> My earliest recollections are that my father would sit on my bedside and rub my back and tell me what a fine boy I was, and almost every night, he would kiss me on the mouth. He was a pro baseball player, a very manly man. But he had no problem expressing his love and blessing to me and to my brother and sister.
>
> My dad died when I was only 14 years old, and he had been sick for about two years before he died. I had a huge hole in my heart. I felt despairing. My mother was very loving and warm, but it just wasn't the same as when my dad was there.
>
> My coach was told that I had lost my father and that it really hit me hard. So every day after workout, he'd stay out with me, and he'd teach me how to play football. He would walk with me after workout to the dressing room with his arm around me. He'd ask me to sit beside him on the bus going out to the game, and he'd just talk to me. Then at noon he'd meet with me, and we'd lift weights for about an hour. I moved from being the slowest, smallest player on the team to, within a year, being unblockable, because I learned good fundamentals. And I didn't even like football then. The only reason I played was because I wanted my father's blessing.[1]

The importance of a father's blessing can't be overstated.

Friends and Brothers

Biblical stories of conflict between brothers don't begin with the patriarchs but with the very first brothers, Cain and Abel. The stories of the patriarchs are filled with brotherly rivalry and also brotherly love. Ishmael and Isaac reunited to bury their

---

[1]Nancy Madison, "The Power of a Father's Blessing," an interview with Bill Glass, *Christianity Today* (January 2006), http://www.christianitytoday.com/ct/2006/001/26.48.html.

father. Esau forgave Jacob, and their relationship was restored. And Joseph forgave his brothers and provided for them for the rest of their lives.

Ali and Baba grew up together. Ali was five years older than Baba. When Ali's parents were killed in a car accident, Baba's father, the judge, adopted Ali into his household:

> Ali and Baba grew up together as childhood play-mates—at least until polio crippled Ali's leg—just like Hassan and I grew up a generation later. Baba was always telling us about the mischief he and Ali used to cause, and Ali would shake his head and say, "But, Agha sahib, tell them who was the architect of the mischief and who the poor laborer?" Baba would laugh and throw his arm around Ali.
>
> But in none of his stories did Baba ever refer to Ali as his friend. (*The Kite Runner*, 21–22)

Once again the son is like the father:

> The curious thing was, I never thought of Hassan and me as friends either. Not in the usual sense, anyhow. Never mind that we taught each other to ride a bicycle with no hands, or to build a fully functional homemade camera out of a cardboard box. Never mind that we spent entire winters flying kites, running kites. Never mind that to me, the face of Afghanistan is that of a boy with a thin-boned frame, a shaved head, and low-set ears, a boy with a Chinese doll face perpetually lit by a harelipped smile.
>
> Never mind any of those things. Because history isn't easy to overcome. Neither is religion. In the end, I was a Pashtun and he was a Hazara, I was Sunni and he was Shi'a, and nothing was ever going to change that. Nothing.
>
> But we were kids who had learned to crawl together, and no history, ethnicity, society, or religion was going to change that either. I spent most of the first twelve years of my life playing with Hassan. Sometimes, my entire childhood seems like one long lazy summer day with Hassan. (*The Kite Runner*, 22)

Amir and Hassan grew up together, inseparable. Because both of them grew up without mothers, the same woman was hired to breastfeed the two boys. Ali told the boys how important this was:

> Then he would remind us that there was a brotherhood between people who had fed from the same breast, a kinship that not even time could break.
>
> Hassan and I fed from the same breasts. We took our first steps on the same lawn in the same year. And, under the same roof, we spoke our first words.
>
> Mine was *Baba*.
>
> His was *Amir*. My name. (*The Kite Runner*, 10)

Whether brother or friend, Amir was sometimes cruel to Hassan, eventually betraying him when he looked on as Hassan was raped. Hassan had proven himself over and over again to Amir, defending him against bullies, encouraging him when his confidence was low, and also filling the role of the servant in preparing his food and doing other household chores. Hassan put up with Amir's occasional cruel taunts and superior attitude. Ultimately, in watching Hassan's rape, Amir could only compare Hassan's look to that of a sacrificial lamb.

Amir, though forgiven by Hassan, was never able to redeem himself with his brother and friend. He did that through his heroic rescue of Hassan's son, Sohrab.

No Old Testament passage comes close to this kind of relationship between brothers and friends. For a biblical parallel we must turn to the New Testament, in which Jesus made friends with people who weren't very popular or respected. In fact, most people would not use the word *friend* for the folks Jesus befriended. He set the example for brothers and friends when he said his disciples were not servants but friends: "No one has greater love than this, to lay down one's life for one's friends...I do not call you servants any longer,...but I have called you friends" (Jn. 15:13–15).

Wives and Mothers

In *The Kite Runner*, as in the stories of the patriarchs, wives and mothers don't seem to play a very prominent role. Yet in both they were very powerful. Sarah convinced Abraham to have a child with her maid Hagar instead of waiting for God to fulfill his promise through her. If she could not give birth to the child herself, she could still maintain her role as the leading female in the household if her maid delivered the heir and first son. Later, having had her own son, Sarah viewed Ishmael and Hagar as a threat rather than an asset. She became cruel to Hagar and Ishmael and eventually insisted that Abraham send them away, which he did, even against his better judgment.

Rebekah plotted with Jacob against Esau to gain the birthright and Isaac's blessing for her favorite son, even though it meant that Jacob must flee for his life from Esau's wrath, never to see his mother again.

Rachel hid her father Laban's household gods from him, deceiving her own father. She was Jacob's favorite over her sister Leah, his first wife; and she died giving birth to Joseph's brother Benjamin.

In *The Kite Runner*, both Amir and Hassan grow up without mothers. Amir's mother died giving birth to him, and he blamed himself for her death. Hassan's mother, we learn, married Ali in an arranged marriage. As soon as Hassan was born, the son of Baba, not Ali, she fled her marriage to a life on the street; and sometimes Hassan heard about his mother in embarrassing and humiliating ways:

> "You! The Hazara! Look at me when I'm talking to you!" the soldier barked. He handed his cigarette to the guy next to him, made a circle with the thumb and index finger of one hand. Poked the middle finger of his other hand through the circle. Poked it in and out. In and out. "I knew your mother, did you know that? I knew her real good. I took her from behind by that creek over there." (*The Kite Runner*, 6)

Surely Hassan's pain was greater than Amir's, thinking that his mother left him because he was born with a deformity and that she preferred the life of a prostitute to being his mother. Much later, when Hassan is married to his wife Farzana, Hassan's mother, Sanaubar, returns home. Whether a type of prodigal or a woman like Hosea's unfaithful wife Gomer, she has known great sin and been disfigured by it, carrying its marks to her grave. But she's come home, seeking forgiveness and a restored relationship.

Hassan, the younger son of promise, struggles at first with the reality of her presence. Then:

> "He took Sanaubar's hand in both of his and told her she could cry if she wanted to but she needn't, she was home now, he said, home with her family. He touched the scars on her face, and ran his hand through her hair." (*The Kite Runner*, 184)

Hassan and Amir both married well. Hassan's wife, Farzana, cared for his mother until her death four years after their son, Sohrab, was born. And Amir's wife, Soraya, cared for his father until he died. But Soraya was unable to have a child. Baba's birthright, the family lineage, would go through his Hazara child, Hassan's son, Sohrab.

DISCUSSION QUESTIONS

---

1. What is our birthright as Christ followers? How is it affected by having brothers and sisters in Christ? How does this impact our relationships with them? How should it affect our witness?

2. Jacob received forgiveness from Esau that was sealed with an embrace. What do you think this meant to Jacob? to Esau? What did it mean to Amir not to be able to ask and receive Hassan's forgiveness, even though he knew Hassan would forgive him? In what ways did Hassan's letter help? In what ways was the letter insufficient?

3. Jacob said that he had seen the face of God and lived. When, if ever, have you felt you saw the "face of God"? Did Amir ever see the "face of God"? If so, when?

4. Do you see Sanaubar more as a Gomer or a prodigal figure? Why?

5. In what ways is Hassan like a sacrificial lamb?

6. Compare Soraya's inability to get pregnant with Sarah's and Rachel's experiences in the Bible. To what did Soraya's family and friends attribute her inability to get pregnant?

For Further Reading

Nancy Madison, "The Power of a Father's Blessing," an interview with Bill Glass, *Christianity Today* (January 2006), available at http://www.christianitytoday.com/ct/2006/001/26.48.html.

CHAPTER 5

Islam

When I was in fifth grade, we had a mullah who taught us about Islam. His name was Mullah Fatiullah Khan, a short, stubby man with a face full of acne scars and a gruff voice. He lectured us about the virtues of zakat and the duty of hadj; he taught us the intricacies of performing the five daily namaz prayers, and made us memorize verses from the Koran—and though he never translated the words for us, he did stress, sometimes with the help of a stripped willow branch, that we had to pronounce the Arabic words correctly so God would hear us better.

(*The Kite Runner*, 14)

Established by the prophet Muhammad in the seventh century C.E., Islam is the youngest of the world's three largest monotheistic religions, along with Judaism and Christianity.[1] Within a century of Muhammad's death (632 C.E.), Islam had spread from India to Spain. The development of Sufi, Islamic mysticism, is credited with helping the religion spread to Africa. Today adherents of Islam may be found in nearly every country, with nearly one person in five worldwide being Muslim. The dominant religion in more than fifty countries, Islam is the principal religion of much of Asia, including Afghanistan. Currently Christianity is the world's largest religion, with approximately 2.1 billion adherents, a third of the world's population. Islam is second with 1.3 billion followers, approximately 21 percent of the population.

---

[1]Information about Islam throughout this chapter is from the Web sites listed on page 104.

The Nature of Islam

In Arabic the word *Islam* means "submission," as the religion focuses on submission to the will of *Allah,* the Arabic word for God. Muslims believe that Islam is the only true faith. Its roots, like those of Judaism and Christianity, go back to Adam and include Noah and Abraham (*Ibrahim*) of the patriarchs in the book of Genesis of the Hebrew Bible. However, where the Judeo-Christian religions focus on the lineage from Abraham to Isaac and then to Jacob, the Muslims move from Abraham to Ishmael (*Isma'il*), Abraham's first son, whose mother was Hagar (Gen. 16.). Other Hebrew Bible figures are also considered prophets of Islam: Moses (*Musa*), who received from God the Torah (*Tawrah*) and David (*Dawud*), who wrote many of the psalms. Jesus (*Isa*), about whom the gospels (*Injil*) were written, is also viewed as a prophet. The final Islamic prophet and the one credited with the fullest revelation of Islam is Muhammad. He is responsible for the Qu'ran (or Koran, as in *The Kite Runner*), which Muslims believe is superior to any other revelation. *Qu'ran* means "recitation," a name chosen to reflect Muhammad's receiving the messages (*suras,* meaning "sections") from the angel Gabriel recorded in the Qu'ran, and being told to recite them to the people.

The Qu'ran is the source of Islamic beliefs and laws (*shari'ah*) and covers every aspect of a Muslim's life—public and private, social and economic, religious and political. The Qu'ran is God's last revelation to man and was delivered to the prophet Muhammad. Muhammad received this word from God in Arabic, so Arabic has always been and continues to be the language of worship for Islam, even though fewer than 15 percent of Muslims today are Arabs.

Islamic laws and beliefs are also informed by three additional sources. (1) The *sunnah* contains the Islamic custom and practice based on Muhammad's words and deeds and is next in importance to the Qu'ran. (2) *Ijma'* expresses the opinions of revered Islamic leaders about concerns not specifically addressed in the Qu'ran. (3) *Qiyas* is the application of the teaching of Islam to situations unknown at the time of the earlier writings.

The history of the followers of Muhammad is one of various groups, or sects, fighting over which one would interpret the

Qu'ran and apply its teachings. During the eighth and ninth centuries Islam developed into a systematized religion. During that time four major schools of thought developed around four Islamic scholars who wrote extensive commentaries about Islamic law (*shari'ah*). Islamic law today continues to be interpreted using these writings. Those who interpret the law in *shari'ah* courts today are called *qadis*, religious judges.

In spite of the emphasis on the sacred writings and the law, Islam is a personal faith between a follower and God. Imams are religious leaders who lead prayers and sermons at the mosque or *masjid*. Before the midday prayers on Fridays the mosque's imam will give a talk on a relevant subject, based on a Qu'ranic text or a story about Muhammad.

Worshipers remove their shoes and perform ritualistic washing before they enter the mosque. Everyone sits or kneels on the floor on small carpets or prayer rugs. Since God cannot be depicted in any way, the worship space is noticeably barren of adornment or decoration. Muslims believe statues or paintings are blasphemous. A niche on the wall, called a *mihrab*, shows the direction the worshipers should face to face Mecca. Many mosques have one or more minarets, tall thin towers. A *muezzin* stands at the top of the tower and calls Muslims to prayer at the five ritual times of the day. In some places women can come to the mosque for worship. When they do, they sit separately from the men out of modesty and to prevent any distraction. It is more common for women to pray and worship at home.

In addition to *imams*, those who pray and preach in a mosque, Islam has religious scholars and mystics called *shaykh* or *mullahs*; religious judges called *qadi*; religious authorities who issue general legal opinions called *mufti*; and other leaders.

The Five Pillars of Islam

Islam's five main requirements of its followers are called the Five Pillars of Islam: (1) the profession of faith (*shahadah*), (2) devotional worship or prayer (*salah*), (3) the religious tax (*zakah*), (4) fasting (*sawm*), and (5) the pilgrimage to Mecca (*hajj*).

1. The profession of faith involves repeating in Arabic the statement, "There is no god but God; Muhammad is the Messenger of God" ("*La ilaha illa Allah; Muhammadun rasul*

Allah"). Although the profession of faith may seem a simple statement, it is packed with meaning, for in repeating it, a Muslim is stating complete compliance and commitment to Islam.

2. Devotional worship or prayer requires Muslims to pray five times a day—at dawn, noon, afternoon, sunset, and evening. For each prayer the Muslim must be facing toward Mecca where the Ka'bah, the House of God, is located. The prayers are ceremonial and both personal and communal. Each prayer requires washing hands, repeating prayers, and bowing a certain number of times. The formula for each prayer is outlined in ritualistic detail.

3. The religious tax (*zakah*) is an obligatory part of worship. The tax encompasses Muslims' social duty to care for those less fortunate—both Muslim and non-Muslim—and is based on a fixed amount. In Muslim countries this tax is generally levied and disbursed by the state, but even where the government is secular and has no system for collecting the tax, individual Muslims are responsible for paying it. The tax does not, however, limit a Muslim's responsibility for helping others financially. They are also expected to give voluntarily the *sadaqah*. This can be compared to the interpretation of Judeo-Christian giving, which includes the tithe, fixed gifts of one-tenth of one's income, and offerings, gifts above and beyond the tithe.

4. Fasting finds its roots in the Qu'ran. Muslims fast to pursue a greater reality of God. A common quote regarding fasting is, "Man has bigger needs than bread." Fasting, too, is ritualized with specific details for how it is done. It is most associated with Ramadan, Islamic holy days that last for a month, beginning with the new moon of the ninth month of the Muslim calendar. Ramadan begins October 16, 2004; October 5, 2005; and September 24, 2006. During the entire time Muslims do not eat or drink from dawn to sunset. The object of the deprivation and abstinence is to subject all human passions and longings to God and to purify oneself to draw closer to God. Fasting, then, is for Muslims

a spiritual discipline, an exercise in controlling and denying self to concentrate on God. During Ramadan, Muslims are also to think of the poor when they feel hungry. In addition to fasting, they are to avoid lying, cheating, cursing, or hurting another person in any way, with the purpose of cultivating compassion for those who are sick or needy. In spite of its strenuous demands, Ramadan is meant to be a celebration. At sunset when they break the fast (*muezzin*), they may worship and enjoy a feast. This celebrative time is more communal than private. In the morning hours, before dawn, men called *musahhirs* beat drums to awaken the faithful to eat before sunrise.

The last ten days of Ramadan are the most sacred because during that time Muslims celebrate the night on which Muhammad received his first revelation from God, called "the Night of Power." On the last day of Ramadan, Muslims believe the favor of God descends. They celebrate this time with a three-day feast (*'Id al-Fitr*). An additional obligatory tax is associated with this feast (*zakat al-fitr*) so the poor may also enjoy this feast time. Sometimes Muslims are unable for health or other reasons to observe all or part of Ramadan. When this happens, they are expected to fast other days to make up for missing the days of Ramadan, and they must give to the needy.

5. The pilgrimage to Mecca (*hajj*) is one of the most moving acts of faith in Islam, often the pinnacle of their faith journey. On that trek they get to see the House of God (*Ka'bah*), the place to which they turn and face each time they pray. According to Muslims this journey dates back to the time of Abraham. Muhammad also made the journey, confirming the practice.

All physically and financially able Muslims are expected to make the pilgrimage at least once in their lives. Pilgrims must make the journey during six days during the twelfth month (*Dhu al-Hijjah*) of the Islamic calendar. Upon arriving in Mecca, pilgrims bathe, cut their hair and nails, remove jewelry and head coverings, and put on the dress of the pilgrim (*ihram*). Everyone wears the same clothing: two white seamless garments that symbolize purity. They pray the *talbiyah:* "Here I am, O God, at thy service." Once prepared and dressed, they enter the *haram*, the area surrounding Mecca, and then Mecca itself. There they circle the House of God. They move from Mecca to Mina where, as they believe Muhammad did, they meditate overnight. The next day all the pilgrims go to Mount Arafat and again pray and meditate. Here they perform "the standing," in which they spend several hours from noon to near sunset in self-examination, supplication, and penance. Muslims believe this part of the *hajj* is the highest point of a Muslim's life and the time when a follower is as close to God as one can be on earth. Some pilgrims go on to the Mount of Mercy where Muhammad is said to have delivered his farewell sermon. After sunset they move on to Muzdalifah where they gather and throw stones at a pillar to signify rejecting evil and Satan. Many believe this is the place where Abraham took his son Ishmael to be sacrificed in obedience to God. (In the Muslim version the son is Ishmael rather than Isaac.)

Pilgrims return to Mina where they sacrifice animals (*'Id al-Adha*). In doing so they celebrate Abraham's willingness to sacrifice his son and commit themselves to to obeying God in all things. Muslims around the world perform identical sacrifices on the same day. Nearing the end of the *hajj*, Muslim pilgrims once again cut their hair. Men trim their hair or shave their heads, and women cut a lock of hair to symbolize their "deconsecration" and return to the world. They remove their special dress and bathe. Once they complete all the essential elements of the pilgrimage, Muslims become *hajjis*.

In Mecca the rites of pilgrimage conclude with Muslims joining in the Circling of the Ka'bah seven times on foot. The intended meaning is that God is at the center of all human existence. After they complete the seventh round, they enter the courtyard of the Mosque at the Place of Abraham to worship where they believe Abraham prayed and built the Ka'bah. While there, they also touch, kiss, or view the Black Stone of the Ka'bah (*Hajar al-Aswad*). They believe this is a fragment of a stone from the original Ka'bah built by Abraham and Ishmael. Some also reenact Hagar's search for water (the *sa'y*) when she and Ishmael were stranded in the valley of Mecca and the angel Gabriel led them to the well of Zamzam.

Beliefs

Muslims believe there is only one God (Allah). God created and rules everything. The heart of faith for Muslims is obedience to God's will. Muslims worship only God because only God is worthy of worship. The primary beliefs about God include the following:

- God is eternal, omniscient, and omnipotent.
- God has always existed and will always exist.
- God knows everything that can be known.
- God can do anything that can be done.
- God has no shape or form, cannot be seen or heard, is neither male nor female.
- God is both just and merciful and rewards and punishes fairly.
- A believer can approach God by praying and by reciting the Qu'ran.
- There is only one God. God has no children, no parents, and no partners.
- God was not created by a being.
- There are no equal, superior, or lesser gods.

They have six main beliefs:

1. Belief in Allah as the one and only God.
2. Belief in angels.
3. Belief in the holy books.
4. Belief in the prophets (Adam, Abraham, Moses, David, Jesus). Muhammad is the final prophet.
5. Belief in the day of judgment, the day when the lives of all human beings will be assessed to decide whether they go to heaven or hell.
6. Belief in predestination, that Allah has already decided what will happen, but this doesn't stop human beings making free choices.

In addition to these beliefs, Muslims are admonished to "commend good and reprimand evil." They are not to gamble, drink, or eat pork. They can eat only meat that has been slaughtered according to their rituals. Although practice varies in different parts of the Muslim world, with the exception of inheritance and witness laws, Islamic rights and obligations apply equally to women and men. The reality of the role of women is more a function of social traditions predating Islam than of actual religious writings.

Jihad, meaning "effort," is the terrifying word coming out of media reports about Islamic terrorists and their holy war against Westerners, Christians, and others. Some sources affirm this definition; others contradict it, saying it is simply misunderstood. Those who disagree with the holy war concept say that *jihad* is a personal, internal struggle with self. The goal of *jihad,* then, is to overcome, to achieve, to attain a goal.

Holy Days

Other than Ramadan, not all Muslims celebrate the same holy days. Two Muslim festivals are established in Islamic law: Eid-ul-Fitr and Eid-ul-Adha (*Eid* or *Id* means "festival"). Muslims celebrate several other special days. For example, some Muslims celebrate the birthday of Muhammad (*pbuh*), and others disapprove of celebrating it on the grounds that it is an innovation, and innovations in religious matters are forbidden because to change suggests that Islam was not complete when Muhammad received his message from God.

Here is a summary of Islamic holy days and when they are celebrated on the Islamic calendar:

Al-Hijra (1 Muharram)—Commemorates the Hijra (or Hegira) in 622 when the Muhammad moved from Mecca to Medina.

Ashura (10 Muharram)—Shi'a Muslims commemorate the martyrdom of Hussein, a grandson of Muhammad in 680. It is a fasting day for Sunni Muslims.

Milad un Nabi (12 Rabi')— Muslims think about Muhammad and the events of his life.

Lailat al Miraj (27 Rajab=Sept. 1, 2005; Aug. 21, 2006)—The festival celebrates Muhammad's journey from Mecca to Jerusalem in one night on a winged creature called Buraq. From Jerusalem he ascended into heaven, where he met the earlier prophets and eventually God.

Lailat-ul-Bara'h (15 Shabaan=Sept. 19, 2005; Sept. 8, 2006)— The Night of Forgiveness (*Lailat-ul-Bara'h*) takes place two weeks before Ramadan. Muslims spend the night in prayer seeking God's guidance and forgiveness for their sins. They put the past behind them and forgive one another. Many Muslims believe that a person's destiny is fixed for the coming year by God on this night.

Lailat al Qadr (27 Ramadan=Oct. 30, 2005; Oct. 19, 2006)—The Night of Power marks the final night in which God revealed the Qu'ran to Muhammad. The Qu'ran was revealed to him in sections (*susas*), not all at once.

Eid ul Fitr (1 Shawwal=Nov. 4, 2005; October 24, 2006)—This marks the end of Ramadan. In Islamic countries it is a public holiday.

Eid ul Adha (10 Dhul-Hijja=Jan. 21, 2005; Jan. 11, 2006)—This festival marks the end of the *hajj* or holy pilgrimage. It is celebrated by all Muslims, not just those who are on the pilgrimage.

Sunni and Shi'a

These two branches of Islam are the largest and most familiar to those outside Islam. Sunni are approximately 90 percent of Muslims worldwide. The division of Islam into these two groups dates back to the death of Muhammad. His followers, approximately 100,000, could not agree on who should follow Muhammad as the leader of Islam.

The larger group, who have become known as Sunni, chose Abu Bakr to succeed him as the next leader (*caliph*). Some sources identify him as a close friend; others say that he was the father of Muhammad's favorite wife. Abu was appointed, but a smaller group, now called the Shiites, believed that Muhammad's son-in-law, Ali, should follow Muhammad. Both groups said their choice was derived from sacred texts.

Ali eventually pledged loyalty to Abu Bakr. Two other caliphs followed Abu, and then Ali was elected caliph. But this led to further dispute because the previous caliph had been murdered. Ali was accused of not bringing the murderers to justice. Many think the divisions were as much political as theological. The theological names given to the groups emerged later: *Sunni* means "one who follows the Sunna," what

Muhammad did and said. *Shi'a* stands for *Shiat Ali,* meaning "partisans of Ali."

Ali's youngest son, Hussein, ruled in Iraq. When Yazid seized the caliphate in 680, Hussein led a rebellion. Hussein was greatly outnumbered but fought heroically and was killed on the battlefield. His death is one of the most significant events in Shi'a history, because Shi´as believe he died for the survival of Shi'a Islam. The remembrance of his death is a holy day commemorated by Shiites today as Ashura, during which millions of pilgrims visit the Imam Hussein mosque in Karbala.

After several centuries a council or *Ulema* was appointed to elect an ayatollah, the supreme spiritual leader. *Ayatollah* means "sign of Allah" and is one who is given great religious authority.

As Sunni Islam expanded, new ethical questions were encountered that demanded religious answers. Sunni Islam responded with four schools of thought: the Hanbali, Hanafi, Maliki, and Shaafii, which to this day continue to seek to find Islamic solutions in any society, regardless of time or place.

In the beginning, the only real difference between Sunni and Shi'a concerned who should lead the Muslim community. Shi'a Muslims have always maintained that Muhammad's family members were the rightful leaders of the Islamic world. Although the Shi'a have always been in the minority among Muslims, they did have their successes. Today Shi'a Islam is seen in the political arena of Iran.

Over time, Shi'a began to turn to *hadith* literature. Sunni do not give prominence to *hadith* over the writings of other scholars. The two sides also fought over whether it was even appropriate to emulate Muhammad. Some thought that to try to act like Muhammad was blasphemous because he was unique. Over time these differences grew. Today Sunni Muslims tend to follow the opinion of the four earliest scholars of the seventh and eight centuries: Hanbali, Hanafi, Maliki, and Shaafii. The Shi'a believe only a living scholar must be followed.

Sunni Muslims pray five times a day, whereas Shi'a Muslims can combine prayers to pray three times a day. Shi'a prayers can often be identified by a small tablet of clay, from a holy place (often Karbala), which is placed on the forehead while prostrating in prayer.

The practice of *muttah,* a temporary marriage, is also permitted in Shi'a Islam, but Sunnis considered it forbidden, as they believe Muhammad abolished it. The relationship and conflict between Sunni and Shi'a Muslims through the ages has shaped contemporary politics wherever the two are found. Like many factions of religious groups, some Muslims show more tolerance than others for one another. Others believe the differences can never be overcome.

> History isn't easy to overcome. Neither is religion. In the end, I was a Pashtun, and he was a Hazara, I was Sunni and he was Shi'a, and nothing was ever going to change that. Nothing." (*The Kite Runner,* 22)

DISCUSSION QUESTIONS

---

1. Basing your opinion on the five pillars of Islam, do you think Islam places more balance on faith/belief or actions/ works, right living or right belief? How does this compare with your perception of the balance in Judaism or Christianity? How is this balance shown in *The Kite Runner*?

2. Every day we see in the media the conflict—played out in violence, politics, and civil unrest—between Muslims over their view of how religion and religious sects should shape government. How does this conflict compare with current and historical conflicts within Judaism or Christianity?

3. *Jihad* is a particular point of disagreement among Muslims. How do you interpret it or understand the term? Is there a parallel in Christianity or Judaism?

For Further Reading

Armstrong, Karen. *Islam: A Short History.* New York: The Modern Library, 2002.

———. *A History of God: The 4,000-Year Quest of Judaism, Christianity and Islam.* New York: Ballantine Books, 1993.

"Glossary of the Middle East." http://www.yourdictionary.com/library/islam.html.

CHAPTER 6

Doing Good, Being Religious

Baba mocks the story behind this Eid, like he mocks everything religious. But he respects the tradition of Eid-e-Qorban. The custom is to divide the meat in thirds, one for the family, one for friends, and one for the poor. Every year, Baba gives it all to the poor. The rich are fat enough already, he says.

(*The Kite Runner*, 67)

The five pillars of Islam are an interesting mixture of doing and believing. The first is professing Islam and proclaiming it aloud, including public prayer and worship. The other pillars include fasting, giving an obligatory offering to help the poor, and making the pilgrimage to Mecca. Is one a Muslim because he or she chooses to follow that religion, because he or she is born in an Islamic state, because he or she claims to be Muslim, because one goes on pilgrimage to Mecca, or because one ends his or her life as a suicide bomber?

Characters in *The Kite Runner* exhibit various beliefs and behavior. Who among the characters is "religious"? And what makes them so—beliefs or behavior? One model for assessing one's faith has been provided by James Fowler and his stages of faith.[1] In 1981 at the time of his first writing about stages of faith, Fowler was—as he remains today—a professor at Emory

---

[1]James W. Fowler, *Stages of Faith: The Psychology of Human Development and the Quest for Meaning* (San Francisco: Harper & Row, 1981). Online, see http://gendertree.com/Stages_of_Faith.htm; http://faculty.plts.edu/gpence/html/fowler.htm.

University's Candler School of Theology in Atlanta. Today he is director of the Center for Research on Faith and Moral Development at Candler and director of Emory's Center for Ethics in Public Policy and the Professions.

Stages of Faith Development

Fowler's theory, based on extensive interviews, is interesting because it applies regardless of religion or belief system. Whether looking at those who profess a monotheistic faith like Christianity, Islam, Judaism, or even Buddhism, Hinduism, or another faith, Fowler says that all people move through at least some of these stages, and a few reach the highest stages. His work is closely aligned with Lawrence Kohlberg's stages of moral development.

Fowler's work is not based only on what people profess to believe, although a belief system is certainly one element of faith as he sees it. But faith is more; for example, it includes one's way of seeing the world—one's worldview. It involves what a person does in life and why, what that person's deepest longings are and how they are fulfilled.

A look at the six stages will clarify Fowler's theory. People in the first three stages depend on an authority outside themselves for their spiritual beliefs—the church, parents, the government, or teachers, for example.

Stage 1. Intuitive-Projective Faith

This is usually the faith of young children who are simply following the beliefs of their parents. They likely see characters in religious stories much as they would the characters of fairy tales or other familiar stories. At this stage children are influenced in their faith by their adult models and their acts of faith such as prayer at meals, telling stories of the faith, church attendance, etc. Imagination and self-awareness are important at this stage of faith.

Stage 2. Mythical-Literal Faith

Children at this stage are beginning to respond to religious figures and worship rituals literally, not abstractly or symbolically.

Stage 3. Synthetic-Conventional Faith

In this stage people tend to conform to the faith of their environment. Their faith involves little self-reflection or differentiation. This is the faith of the masses. Most people stop their journey of faith development at this stage. At this stage some questioning occurs, but answers that satisfy are those of the greatest authority figures or influencing groups rather than answers sought through research and study, prayer, and reflection. For example, at this stage a person might encounter a conflict between creation and evolution, which might be resolved by what a faith community or authority figure says is true. This is not to say that beliefs at this stage are not deeply held; they can be. But they are not based on great consideration of options; they are largely based on what others say is true. Acceptance of the group and being a part of the group means conforming to the group's belief structure.

Stage 4. Individuative-Reflective Faith

People at this stage are no longer dependent on an external belief system. They are not limited to or bound by the beliefs of others. People at this stage of faith no longer look to an external authority but look inward to determine the direction of their faith. At this stage a person will no longer conform to a group in matters of belief, whether family; friends; or a faith group such as a church, synagogue, or mosque. At this stage a person will determine beliefs, values, and faith relationships based on self-reflection rather than on what an outside authority figure says. People at this stage are taking responsibility for their own beliefs, how they will develop, and how they will affect their lifestyle.

Stage 5. Conjunctive Faith

Building on stage 4, people here move beyond their self-reflection and forming of their own faith. No longer dependent for their faith on a specific set of beliefs or codes, they become more tolerant of others' beliefs even though such beliefs may differ radically from their own. People at this stage begin to think more about putting their faith into action than simply about what they believe.

Stage 6. Universalizing Faith

Few people reach this stage. Most who do are senior adults. People at this stage tend to focus on universal values such as unconditional love and justice. That focus means self-sacrifice, including one's life if necessary. Examples often given of people at this stage in their faith walk include Mother Teresa and Mahatma Gandhi.

After this brief look at Fowler's stages of faith, some scenes in *The Kite Runner* can be understood in the context of faith stage or faith development.

Amir and Hassan had religious influences beginning shortly after their birth when the woman who nursed both of them sang:

> On a high mountain I stood,
> And cried the name of Ali, Lion of God.
> O, Ali, Lion of God, King of Men,
> Bring joy to our sorrowful hearts. (*The Kite Runner*, 10)

Consider this exchange between Baba and Amir:

> Baba saw the world in black and white. And he got to decide what was black and what was white...
>
> When I was in fifth grade, we had a mullah who taught us about Islam...He lectured us about the virtues of *zakat* and the duty of *hadj;* he taught us the intricacies of performing the five daily *namaz* prayers, and made us memorize verses from the Koran...He told us one day that Islam considered drinking a terrible sin...
>
> We were upstairs in Baba's study...I told him what Mullah Fatiullah Khan had taught us in class. Baba was pouring himself a whiskey from the bar...Then he lowered himself into the leather sofa, put down his drink, and propped me up on his lap...I couldn't decide whether I wanted to hug him or leap from his lap in mortal fear.
>
> "I see you've confused what you're learning in school with actual education," he said in his thick voice.
>
> "But if what he said is true then does it make you a sinner, Baba?"...
>
> "Do you want to know what your father thinks about sin?"

"Yes."...

"Now, no matter what the mullah teaches, there is only one sin, only one. And that is theft. Every other sin is a variation of theft. Do you understand that?" (*The Kite Runner*, 14–16).

It's pretty clear that Amir is in one of the earlier stages of faith. He has a conflict between authority figures and is trying to decide which one he will accept. This is confirmed at the kite-fighting contest. He thinks about God but only how God, if God is real, can meet his own selfish desires:

Caught between Baba and the mullahs at school, I still hadn't made up my mind about God. But when a Koran *ayat* I had learned in my *diniyat* class rose to my lips, I muttered it...

If Baba was wrong and there *was* a God like they said in school, then He'd let me win. (*The Kite Runner*, 55, 57)

By the time they reach America and Baba becomes ill, when Amir is in his late teens, he has perhaps become less selfish, praying for his father instead of himself. Yet this depends on his motives. Praying for his father could still be a selfish prayer. But it is evident that Amir has another clash of realities and is still trying to determine what and whom he believes about faith:

That night, I waited until Baba fell asleep, and then folded a blanket. I used it as a prayer rug. Bowing my head to the ground, I recited half-forgotten verses from the Koran—verses the mullah had made us commit to memory in Kabul—and asked for kindness from a God I wasn't sure existed. I envied the mullah now, envied his faith and certainty. (*The Kite Runner*, 135)

The next time we see Amir at prayer he is in the hospital waiting to see whether Sohrab will live or die. The last time he had prayed was fifteen years earlier when Baba was sick:

I throw my makeshift *jai-namaz*, my prayer rug, on the floor and I get on my knees, lower my forehead to the ground, my tears soaking through the sheet. I bow to the west. Then I remember I haven't prayed for over fifteen years. I have long forgotten the words. But it doesn't matter. I will utter those few words I still remember: *La illaha il Allah. Muhammad u rasul ullah.* There is no God but Allah and Muhammad is His messenger. I see now that Baba was wrong, there is a God, there always had been. I see Him here, in the eyes of the people in this corridor of desperation. This is the real house of God, this is where those who have lost God will find Him, not the white *masjid* with its bright diamond lights and towering minarets. There is a God, there has to be, and now I will pray, I will pray that He forgive that I have neglected Him all of these years, forgive that I have betrayed, lied, and sinned with impunity only to turn to Him now in my hour of need, I pray that He is as merciful, benevolent, and gracious as His book says He is. I bow to the west and kiss the ground and promise that I will do *zakat,* I will do *namaz,* I will fast during Ramadan and when Ramadan has passed I will go on fasting. I will commit to memory every last word of His holy book, and I will set on a pilgrimage to that sweltering city in the desert and bow before the Ka'bah too. I will do all of this and I will think of Him every day from this day on if He only grants me this one wish: My hands are stained with Hassan's blood; I pray God doesn't let them get stained with the blood of his boy too.

I hear a whimpering and realize it is mine, my lips are salty with the tears trickling down my face. I feel the eyes of everyone in this corridor on me and still I bow to the west. I pray. I pray that my sins have not caught up with me the way I'd always feared they would. (*The Kite Runner,* 301–2)

This is the first time Amir has prayed with certainty that God is real. He prays with abandon, not worrying about what those around him think. For the first time he cares about God's opinion of him instead of his opinion of God. Although he may in some ways be bargaining with God, he is sincerely praying for another person. His prayer can certainly be compared with that of David, praying for God to let his firstborn son live—his child with Bathsheba, the son of his sin. Amir has finally broken free of a conforming faith to one he owns for himself.

And what of Baba's faith? While he denies being "religious," he doesn't really deny having faith, belief in God. He keeps religious holidays and goes beyond what is required. He gives sacrificially, building an orphanage and risking his life by confronting a Russian guard to defend a woman he didn't really know. Amir's wedding in America, where surely he could have had a secular wedding if Baba had disdained religion as much as he claimed, was performed by a mullah. Even the end of his life gave evidence of faith, with people speaking of his kindnesses and the Koran being read. Baba had faith, but not a faith that conformed.

Others in the book give evidence of faith (though there is hardly enough information to ascribe a faith state). Ali, in his quiet way, stands out as an example of a kind man, a man of faith. To help his family he married a woman of questionable reputation. This might not matter to some men, but Ali was a man of faith, having committed the Koran to memory. He prayed regularly for the son that wasn't really his and told him so.

Rahib Khan also offers a religious model. Sensitive to others, kind, and one who sought to facilitate reconciliation and peace, he talks with Amir about God's will and continues his ritual praying even in his dying days.

As unpleasant as it is to consider the issue at all, the question of Assef's faith must be addressed. Early in life, like the other boys, he is highly influenced by his father. This is seen, for example, in his admiration of Adolf Hitler and in his disdain of Hazaras. Yet he was schooled alongside Amir and knew the teachings of the mullahs. In his self-centeredness he couldn't see his wrongdoing even in raping Hassan, for he said, "There's nothing sinful about teaching a lesson to a disrespectful donkey."

In adulthood, according to Fowler's theory, Assef may have actually moved to stage 4 faith, which can also be self-centered, because he has chosen what he will and will not believe. He forgives—or dismisses completely—his ongoing sin of abusing young boys and his drug use, clearly sins in the strict Islamic law he spent his life enforcing. He even took pride in the mass killing of the Hazara, saying:

> "You don't know the meaning of the word 'liberating' until you've done that, stood in a roomful of targets, let the bullets fly, free of guilt and remorse, knowing you are virtuous, good, and decent. Knowing you're doing God's work. It's breathtaking." (*The Kite Runner*, 242)

If not for his explanation (confession?) to Amir about how he came to be involved with the Taliban, it would be easy to claim he had no faith. But he said:

> "As you may remember, I wasn't much of a religious type. But one day I had an epiphany. I had it in jail...
>
> "Every night the commandant, a half-Hazara, half-Uzbek thing who smelled like a rotting donkey, would have one of the prisoners dragged out of the cell and he'd beat him until sweat poured from his fat face...One night he picked me. It couldn't have come at a worse time. I'd been peeing blood for three days. Kidney stones...It's the worst imaginable pain...They dragged me out and he started kicking me...I was screaming and screaming and he kept kicking me and then, suddenly, he kicked me on the left kidney and the stone passed. Just like that!...I started laughing. He got mad and hit me harder, and the harder he kicked me, the harder I laughed...I kept laughing and laughing because suddenly I knew that had been a message from God: He was on *my* side. He wanted me to live for a reason...
>
> "I've been on a mission ever since...
>
> "Afghanistan is like a beautiful mansion littered with garbage, and someone has to take out the garbage." (*The Kite Runner*, 247–48)

Assef undoubtedly had a faith, but one that is repugnant to many people. But his faith leads us to look at the Taliban as a whole. The Taliban is a fundamentalist Islamic militia who in 1996 took over rule of Afghanistan after the civil war that ensued when Russia left the country. The Afghan people welcomed their rule because of the harsh and corrupt conditions under the communist warlords. When the Taliban militia took over Afghanistan, they imposed an Islamic government in Kabul and enforced their interpretation of a strict Muslim code of behavior. Can an entire religious group have a stage of faith? If so, the Taliban's faith is stuck at stage 3 in Fowler's hierarchy. The Taliban is all about authority and conformity. Public hangings and stonings for major infractions such as adultery, beatings for acts like talking too loud, flying a kite, or cheering at a soccer game show the Taliban's control of day-to-day life in order to ensure that everyone conform to their interpretation of Islam. When a government or any group of people forces its view of religion on others, it will retard the spiritual growth of the entire society—though not of every individual—if not stop it all together. But can a society have a stage of faith forced on them?

Black and White and Shades of Gray

Although using a framework such as Fowler's provides one way of looking at faith and one way of understanding people's faith journeys, in many ways it is inevitably less than completely satisfying. It moves people along a continuum that allows people to get stuck and never progress, but it doesn't provide for a significant faith event that could reset or completely redirect one's faith journey—such as a conversion experience. While it may fall short, it does allow us to look at a variety of types of faith in a comparative context.

Fowler's framework also provides a way of seeing why some people believe everyone should conform to their rules of faith, while other people are more tolerant of others' beliefs. In Fowler's model the mullahs model a lower faith stage, a system in which lack of conformity means exclusion at best—and death for punishment at worst—in response to failing to conform. Children may be taught rules, but not all societies strictly enforce all the rules. The strict execution of meting out the punishment for all infractions is seldom seen in non-Islamic governments. But as clearly seen in the acts of the Taliban in *The Kite Runner*, as well as in the nightly news, such enforcement is carried out by an Islamic state. Only in a system at a lower level of faith development would a man be declared mentally incompetent for choosing another religion, an event that received worldwide attention in March 2006, when, under Afghanistan's new "democratic" but Islamic government, a man was found guilty of converting from Islam to Christianity, an offense punishable by death.

Extremists of any faith have little tolerance of beliefs and lifestyles that deviate from their own. People with a less extremist view of faith tend to be less judgmental of those who do not live by a set of standards, even if they themselves have chosen to live by those standards. In Fowler's framework, such people have arrived at a higher level of faith. Of course, nothing is this clear-cut and simple. People could be more tolerant because the lower levels of faith in their community are less structured by rules, so tolerance may reflect the norm of their authority figures or peers rather than mean a more highly developed faith.

A framework such as this also makes it impossible to ascertain motives. For example, if people act altruistically, they may have a variety of motivations for doing so. They may help others because it is part of the belief system of their faith community, so even in a conforming faith, the model is to do good deeds for others. Or an individual may be acting out of a personal faith that, like stage 1, is somewhat self-centered, perhaps doing good out of fear, guilt, or a desire for praise rather than a real outgrowth of a personalized faith.

A simple case of mistaken motives occurs in *The Kite Runner* when Amir is on his way back to Afghanistan and stops for the night at the home of relatives of his driver, Farid. Amir saw the children staring at his watch, or so he thought, and gave it to them. Later he realized that he was eating their food. Because he was a guest, he had received not only their best but all they had. The children were staring because they were hungry. Amir could not easily recognize motives he had never experienced.

The bottom line is that motives are complex. Though people are commonly judged by their actions, and motivations are often attached to what people do, actions alone are not enough to discern motivation, thought processes, the reasons behind the actions. Baba is an interesting case study. As a boy, Amir sees Baba as having clearly defined notions about everything: "Baba saw the world in black and white. And he got to decide what was black and what was white" (*The Kite Runner*, 14). Was that only a boy's perspective, or had Amir already grasped the truth about Baba?

Baba seemed to struggle with what he thought about his son, Amir. To have a model for how his son should be and to want to force that model on his son tends to support a black-and-white mind-set. But did he struggle because he wanted his son to be more like him or because of a complex mixture of feelings of love and guilt involving his relationship with Hassan and his feelings about the death of Amir's mother?

He said he wasn't religious, and he didn't obey all the religious rules, such as abstaining from alcoholic beverages; but he went beyond what was required in helping those less fortunate. This may have met his own personalized code of ethics, but it did not conform to society's requirements. Was his motive for building the orphanage, and later for defending the woman, one of guilt or of love?

Baba grew up with Ali and clearly cared about him, but did he really do anything to help those who were of another ethnic group or religious subgroup? Would he have claimed Hassan as his own son if the mother had been Pashtun? Perhaps Baba did see things in black and white and couldn't overcome them to face losing standing in the community or challenging what was accepted in society, which was, after all, the conformity of Islam and its ethnic minorities and sects.

Some people believe that ultimately no one does anything without a selfish motive. They may do good out of guilt or just the satisfying feeling they get when they help others. If the only reason for helping others is bragging rights or the good feeling the doer gets, the motivation is self-centered and self-serving. Jesus said that such behavior is its own reward:

> "Beware of practicing your piety before others in order to be seen by them; for then you have no reward from your Father in heaven.
>
> "So whenever you give alms, do not sound a trumpet before you, as the hypocrites do in the synagogues and in the streets, so that they may be praised by others. Truly I tell you, they have received their reward. But

when you give alms, do not let your left hand know
what your right hand is doing, so that your alms may
be done in secret; and your Father who sees in secret
will reward you." (Mt. 6:1–4)

Evangelical Christians have consistently challenged Fowler's
faith stages because he does not include a specific moment of
decision. Not only that, but the faith stages seem to indicate
that progression is up to the individual alone. A verse essential
to their argument is Ephesians 2:8: "For by grace you have been
saved through faith, and this is not your own doing; it is the
gift of God—not the result of works, so that no one may boast."
But Christ followers *are* encouraged to put their faith into action:

What good is it, my brothers and sisters, if you say you
have faith but do not have works? Can faith save you?
If a brother or sister is naked and lacks daily food, and
one of you says to them, "Go in peace; keep warm and
eat your fill," and yet you do not supply their bodily
needs, what is the good of that? So faith by itself, if it
has no works, is dead. (Jas. 2:14–17)

James, Jesus' brother, was echoing what he had heard Jesus
teach. In the Sermon on the Mount, Jesus said that people are
known by their actions: "Thus you will know them by their
fruits" (Mt. 7:20). Paul later spelled out what those fruits are:
"The fruit of the Spirit is love, joy, peace, patience, kindness, gen-
erosity, faithfulness, gentleness, and self-control" (Gal. 5:22–23).

Also in the Sermon on the Mount, Jesus warned about
judging others and told his listeners that people are known by
their actions, whether good or bad. "Do not judge, so that you
may not be judged. For with the judgment you make you will
be judged, and the measure you give will be the measure you
get. Why do you see the speck in your neighbor's eye, but do
not notice the log in your own eye?" (Mt. 7:1–4). Such a concept
was beyond Assef's thinking. His actions, as well as his words,
indicate that he believed that God had given him both the power
and the right to use that power in whatever way he saw fit.
Apparently God had given him the right to live an immoral
lifestyle both publicly and privately.

Jesus was not without critics. The Pharisees were all about laws and not about love or tolerance. They criticized Jesus for spending time with sinners and for feeding and healing folks on the Sabbath. Most good works seemed to draw negative comments. Baba was criticized for spending money on orphans or for risking his life to defend the woman at the border crossing. Selfish people often feel threatened by those who do good.

Similarly, in the Old Testament, God was not pleased with ritualistic worship that kept the format but lost the feeling. Such acts of worship were empty, showing little love for God and less for fellow human beings. God cares about both actions and motives: "He has told you, O mortal, what is good; / and what does the LORD require of you / but to do justice, and to love kindness, / and to walk humbly with your God?" (Mic. 6:8).

And in Amos:

"I hate, I despise your festivals,
      and I take no delight in your solemn assemblies.
Even though you offer me your burnt offerings and grain
      offerings,
      I will not accept them;
and the offerings of well-being of your fatted animals
      I will not look upon.
Take away from me the noise of your songs;
      I will not listen to the melody of your harps.
But let justice roll down like waters,
      and righteousness like an ever-flowing stream.
                                        (Am. 5:21–23)

In the New Testament we read that love should be the greatest motive. In the gospel of John, we read Jesus' words:

"As the Father has loved me, so I have loved you; abide in my love. If you keep my commandments, you will abide in my love, just as I have kept my Father's commandments and abide in his love. I have said these things to you so that my joy may be in you, and that your joy may be complete.

"This is my commandment, that you love one another as I have loved you. No one has greater love than this, to lay down one's life for one's friends." (Jn. 15:9–13)

Then in the first letter of John, he wrote: "In this is love, not that we loved God but that he loved us and sent his Son to be the atoning sacrifice for our sins. Beloved, since God loved us so much, we also ought to love one another" (1 Jn. 4:10–11).

Paul wrote about a maturing faith, built on the motivation of love, that reaches out to others: "If I speak in the tongues of mortals and of angels, but do not have love, I am a noisy gong or a clanging cymbal…Love never ends…The greatest of these is love" (1 Cor. 13:1, 8a, 13b). Peter also encouraged Christ followers to mature in their faith: "Grow in the grace and knowledge of our Lord and Savior Jesus Christ" (2 Pet. 3:18).

And Paul wrote to the Philippians: "Therefore, my beloved, just as you have always obeyed me, not only in my presence, but much more now in my absence, work out your own salvation with fear and trembling" (Phil. 2:12)—mature and grow but be careful how you do it. Paul also encouraged people to obey the old laws even though grace had freed them from such restrictions lest they become a stumbling block for those with less mature faith. For example, when talking about eating food sacrificed to idols, Paul said there was nothing wrong with eating it except that if doing so offends a new believer: "If food is a cause of their falling, I will never eat meat, so that I may not cause one of them to fall" (1 Cor. 8:13).

And James wrote:

> Who is wise and understanding among you? Show by your good life that your works are done with gentleness born of wisdom. But if you have bitter envy and selfish ambition in your hearts, do not be boastful and false to the truth. Such wisdom does not come down from above, but is earthly, unspiritual, devilish. For where there is envy and selfish ambition, there will also be disorder and wickedness of every kind. But the wisdom from above is first pure, then peaceable, gentle, willing to yield, full of mercy and good fruits, without a trace of partiality or hypocrisy. And a harvest of righteousness is sown in peace for those who make peace. (Jas. 3:13–18)

Christ followers are to mature in their faith by obeying Jesus' teachings, giving evidence of their faith by their actions, and cultivating good motives for all they do.

DISCUSSION QUESTIONS

1. John Westerhoff also developed a theory of faith development[2] with fewer steps that is somewhat less complex than Fowler's. His theory looks at faith as a journey with four styles rather than stages: (1) affective, the experienced faith of childhood; (2) affiliative faith, with an emphasis on belonging to a faith community; (3) search faith, which includes doubts, judgments, and experimentation; and (4) owned faith, which a person has examined and claimed as part of one's personal identity. Using Westerhoff's definition, how would you describe the faith of Amir, Baba, Assef, and the Taliban?

2. The Taliban's is a faith of fear. Does fear have a role in other kinds of faith? If so, what is it?

3. In Afghanistan during the Taliban control, when people flew kites even though it was against the law, was their daring merely risky protest behavior, or could it possibly be interpreted as an act of faith?

4. Is it easier to stay at Fowler's stage 3 and conform, accepting the faith of the ruling authority and the faith community, or is it better to risk alienation or worse to struggle with issues that are clear-cut at stage 3? For example, would people of faith at stage 3 always be satisfied with acts like segregation? Would believers have to move to stage 4 to struggle with the implications of faith to deal with such social issues?

5. Can a religion or a denomination have a dominant faith stage? If so, give examples. Can any large group ever move past Fowler's stage 3?

---

[2]John H. Westerhoff, *Will Our Children Have Faith?* (Harrisburg, Pa.: Morehouse, 2000).

6. Do people at Fowler's stage 3, conforming faith, act on behalf of others' welfare, or does such behavior come only at a higher stage of faith?

7. Which comes first, motivation or action? If motivation is not right, should acts of kindness be done? Can doing good deeds lead to having a better motivation?

8. Baba saw everything in black and white, but he determined what was black and white. He could make up the rules as he went along, his rules. When people mature in their faith or gain wisdom, do the rules change? Do their expectations of conforming to rules change? How does this impact other people?

For Further Reading

Fowler, James W. *Stages of Faith: The Psychology of Human Development*. San Francisco: Harper & Row, 1981.

Westerhoff, John H. *Will Our Children Have Faith?* Harrisburg, Pa.: Morehouse, 2000.

CHAPTER 7

From Sin and Suffering to Freedom in Finding Forgiveness

It was only a smile, nothing more. It didn't make everything all right. It didn't make anything all right. Only a smile. A tiny thing…

But I'll take it. With open arms. Because when spring comes, it melts the snow one flake at a time, and maybe I just witnessed the first flake melting.

I ran. A grown man running with a swarm of screaming children. But I didn't care. I ran with the wind blowing in my face, and a smile as wide as the Valley of Panjsher on my lips.

(*The Kite Runner*, 324)

Eric Liddell was a missionary to China. He was also an Olympic gold medal winner for Great Britain in 1924. The movie *Chariots of Fire* tells the story of how his faith and his running came together as he took a public stand for obeying the Ten Commandments. His main race at the Olympic Games was to take place on Sunday. Liddell would not compete on the Lord's Day. He feared that his running on Sunday might lead astray some of the young boys and men who looked up to him. Liddell believed his ability to run fast was a gift from God, and he said he felt God's pleasure when he ran. To run on Sunday would have robbed God of the worship due him.

By the end of this chapter, Amir will feel God's pleasure when he runs, but we must deal with his sin, suffering, and guilt before he finds forgiveness.

Theft—the Only Sin

Reducing all sins to just one eliminates the need to memorize the entire Ten Commandments, the golden rule, or the greatest commandment, but it doesn't simplify the law. Let's take a closer look, first at the Ten Commandments.

1. "You shall have no other gods before me" (Ex. 20:3). Placing anything ahead of God robs him of the "first place" position he demands and deserves.

2. "You shall not make for yourself an idol" (Ex. 20:4). Worshiping any object steals God's singular position as the only recipient of our love and devotion and places what was created ahead of the Creator.

3. "You shall not make wrongful use of the name of the LORD your God" (Ex. 20:7). Using God's name inappropriately robs God of the respect his name should elicit.

4. "Remember the sabbath day, and keep it holy" (Ex. 20:8). After creation God instituted the Sabbath to rest from his labor and to reflect on the good work that he had done. Failure to reflect on God on the Sabbath robs God of the obedience due him and of gratitude for his creative and sustaining power.

5. "Honor your father and your mother" (Ex. 20:12). Failure to honor parents robs them of respect and ultimately robs parents and children of having a good relationship with each other. Breaking this commandment also means failing to obey God as Father, also robbing him of obedience and respect.

6. "You shall not murder" (Ex. 20:13). Murder robs a person of life and, like all sin, robs the murderer of an intimate relationship with God.

7. "You shall not commit adultery" (Ex. 20:14). Adultery robs those who break this commandment of an open, honest relationship with their marriage partners and with God. It robs the marriage partners of trust and love. It robs God of honoring the home, the first institution he created.

In breaking this commandment—having a sexual relationship with Ali's wife, Sanaubar—Baba began a spiral of sin that affected his life, the lives of those around him, and subsequent generations. He robbed Sanaubar and Ali of a relationship that never had a chance to develop. He may have robbed Sanaubar of a home and self-respect. He robbed himself of an open and honest relationship with both his sons and his sons of having a relationship as brothers. He robbed Ali of trust. He robbed Hassan of a mother.

8. "You shall not steal" (Ex. 20:15). According to Baba, the only commandment needed. Amir chose this commandment to implicate Hassan because he knew it was the sin his father hated most. Indeed he had heard his father say, "There is no act more wretched than stealing, Amir…A man who takes what's not his to take, be it a life or a loaf of *naan*…I spit on such a man. And if I ever cross paths with him, God help him. Do you understand?" (*The Kite Runner*, 16). Amir was threatening to take the life of one who committed theft, the sin he had committed in breaking the seventh commandment. Although Baba quickly forgave Hassan of the wrong he took upon himself, even though he had done no wrong, Amir's action robbed the boys and men of the opportunity for relationship to be restored, separating the pairs of fathers and sons for the rest of their lives.

9. "You shall not bear false witness against your neighbor" (Ex. 20:16). Lying about others robs them of their dignity, reputation, self-esteem, and more. It may rob them of relationships, occupation, or even life itself. To extend this commandment, failure to speak the truth robs people of healthy relationships. This was Amir's sin in driving Hassan and Ali away. To cover his own sin, he lied about others.

10. "You shall not covet" (Ex. 20:17). Wanting what other people have robs the person breaking this commandment of the joy of living. Amir was jealous of anyone who got Baba's attention and approval. Feeling that he did not measure up to Baba's expectations, he coveted those who pleased his father. He even coveted Hassan's harelip and surgery if it could have brought his distant father closer.

In the New Testament, Jesus regularly affirmed the importance of the Ten Commandments. In the Sermon on the Mount, he said:

> "Do not think that I have come to abolish the law or the prophets; I have come not to abolish but to fulfill. For truly I tell you, until heaven and earth pass away, not

one letter, not one stroke of a letter, will pass from the law until all is accomplished. Therefore, whoever breaks one of the least of these commandments, and teaches others to do the same, will be called least in the kingdom of heaven; but whoever does them and teaches them will be called great in the kingdom of heaven." (Mt. 5:17–19)

When a scribe asked Jesus which commandment is the most important, he didn't say theft. Jesus responded by quoting the *shema* (Deut. 6:4–5), the first or greatest commandment, and adding a positive summary of the commandments about human relationships with one another:

"The first is, 'Hear, O Israel: the Lord our God, the Lord is one; you shall love the Lord your God with all your heart, and with all your soul, and with all your mind, and with all your strength.' The second is this, 'You shall love your neighbor as yourself.' There is no other commandment greater than these." (Mk. 12:29–31)

Jesus also talked about loving others in his Sermon on the Mount, in what has come to be called the golden rule: "In everything do to others as you would have them do to you; for this is the law and the prophets" (Mt. 7:12). Failure to love God with your whole self robs God of first place in your life. Failure to love others as much as you love yourself, to treat them as you would like to be treated, robs others of relationship and respect.

Ultimately the one who breaks any of these commandments is the one who suffers most. Breaking any of the commandments means robbing oneself of self-respect, peace of mind, a clear conscience, and healthy relationships with one another and with God. God's law is ultimately for our own good. We rob ourselves of feeling God's pleasure when we break his law.

Suffering

A child doesn't need too many experiences of being teased and taunted to learn that the rhyme, "Sticks and stones may break my bones, but words will never hurt me," is simply not true. Words hurt. Physical pain hurts. Suffering comes in all sorts of forms—mental, emotional, physical, spiritual. All of these are evident in *The Kite Runner*.

Hassan is most often the recipient. He's teased by other children because of his harelip, because of his father's limp, and because his mother has become a prostitute. But often Hassan's pain is inflicted by Amir. Especially after the rape, Amir, in his own pain, lashes out at Hassan. " 'I want you to stop harassing me. I want you to go away,' I snapped" (*The Kite Runner*, 77).

Amir wanted Hassan to respond in kind, hoping that would lessen his pain, but Hassan never retaliated. One day Amir pummeled Hassan with pomegranates until Hassan was covered with the blood-red juice. Still Hassan refused to fight back.

Hassan's response was one of meekness—strength under control—not of cowardice. He had already proved his courage when he defended Amir against the bullies led by Assef.

But Hassan is not the only one in pain in *The Kite Runner*. The reader doesn't understand until the end of the book that Baba is tormented by his guilt and his secrets. And Amir may suffer the most because of his guilt—guilt over disappointing his father, being responsible for the death of his mother, betraying Hassan by not coming to his rescue, and driving away Ali and Hassan through a lie.

Much of this suffering is more mental and emotional than physical, but the book is filled with physical suffering as well—Hassan's rape, Baba's and Rahim Kahn's cancer, the hunger of the children, the torturous acts of the Taliban, the mistreatment of the orphans, the killings of the Hazaras, and Sohrab's attempted suicide. Even flying kites is a physically painful experience, with the glass-coated string continually cutting into the flyers' fingers and palms.

But the physical suffering in the book culminates in the two beatings near the end of the book—Assef's beating when he is in jail and Amir's beating from Assef in trying to get Sohrab. In their pain and suffering, both men find release. Assef laughed because he believed God had used the boot of his torturer to give him release from the pain of the kidney stone. He responded with retaliation against the one who beat him by pursuing a mission to purify Afghanistan of ethnic and religious minorities.

Amir, on the other hand, laughed because he had at last found peace:

> For the first time since the winter of 1975, I felt at peace. I laughed because I saw that, in some hidden nook in a corner of my mind, I'd even been looking forward to this. I remembered the day on the hill I had pelted Hassan with pomegranates and tried to provoke him. He'd just stood there, doing nothing, red juice soaking through his shirt like blood. Then he'd taken the pomegranate from my hand, crushed it against his forehead. *Are you satisfied now?* he'd hissed. *Do you feel better?* I hadn't been happy and I hadn't felt better, not at all. But I did now. My body was broken—just how badly I wouldn't find out until later—but I felt *healed*. Healed at last. I laughed. (*The Kite Runner*, 252–53)

Suffering has a variety of meanings and evokes different responses from people. It's a topic all religions address because of the reoccurring question of why God allows people to suffer.

Suffering is at the heart of the Christian faith, for Christ followers believe that God sent his blameless, perfect Son to take on the sins of the world and to suffer and die a painful death to redeem those who believe in him. In the worldwide natural disasters of 2004–2005, some Christians saw God's punishment; other Christians totally rejected this concept. Rather, they saw such events as tests of the faith, giving believers in the midst of a crisis the strength to endure, and giving believers outside the catastrophe an opportunity to respond in caring for those less fortunate. Paul wrote, "We also boast in our sufferings, knowing that suffering produces endurance, and endurance produces character, and character produces hope, and hope does not disappoint us, because God's love has been poured into our hearts through the Holy Spirit that has been given to us" (Rom. 5:3–5).

Some Christians believe that even when innocent people suffer, God is working to some greater good, basing their belief on passages such as Romans 8:28: "We know that all things work together for good for those who love God."[1]

The late Pope John Paul II experienced great suffering in his later years and humbly and publicly endured the pain. He spoke about suffering on the World Day of the Sick in 2002:

> The answer to the question of the meaning of suffering has been "given by God to man in the Cross of Jesus Christ." Suffering, a consequence of original sin, takes on a new meaning; it becomes a sharing in the saving work of Jesus Christ (cf. *Catechism of the Catholic Church*, 1521). Through His suffering on the Cross, Christ has prevailed over evil and enables us too to overcome it. Our sufferings become meaningful and precious when united with His. As God and man, Christ has taken upon Himself the sufferings of humanity, and in Him human suffering itself takes on a redemptive meaning. In this union between the human and the divine, suffering brings forth good and overcomes evil. In expressing my profound solidarity with all those who are suffering, I earnestly pray that the celebration of the World Day of the Sick will be for them a providential moment opening a new horizon of meaning in their lives.[2]

Dr. Muzammil H. Siddiqi, director of the Islamic Society of Orange County and president of the Islamic Society of North America, offers this about suffering:

> Sufferings occur to teach us that we must adhere to Allah's natural and moral laws. It is sometimes to punish those who violate Allah's natural or moral laws. It is to test our faith in Allah and to test our commitment to human values and charity. Whenever we encounter suffering we should ask ourselves, "Have we broken any law of Allah?" Let us study the cause of the problem

---

[1]Ellen Leventry, "Why Bad Things Happen," on Beliefnet site, http://www.beliefnet.com/story/158/story_15870_1.html.

[2]Pope John Paul II, "The Christian Response to Suffering," http://www.wf-f.org/02-1-ChristianSuffering.html.

and use the corrective methods. "Could it be a punishment?" Let us repent and ask forgiveness and reform our ways. "Could it be a test and trial for us?" Let us work hard to pass this test.

Believers face the sufferings with prayers, repentance and good deeds. The non-believers face the sufferings with doubts and confusions. They blame Allah or make arguments against Him.[3]

The word *Islam* means "submission." Many Muslims believe that submission includes suffering; enduring pain is a way of submitting to God's will. Some suffering is Satan's work, carried out by *jinn,* Satan's cohorts. God allows suffering as a test of faith. Many Muslims believe that through suffering their faith grows stronger; pain leads to repentance, prayer, and good deeds. In the Qu'ran, natural disasters are often God's punishment on groups of people.[4]

Hassan consistently submitted to suffering. Most of his life Amir avoided suffering and pain, but in going to Afghanistan to find Sohrab and ultimately in facing Assef again, he finally submitted, and in his submission he became victorious. For Amir the pain of possibly losing Sohrab did lead to repentance, prayer, and good deeds.

Guilt

Like a genetic part of his makeup, Amir seems to have been born with the inherited guilt of his father. When he was young, he took the blame for his mother's death and believed this was the root of his father's problem with him:

> I always felt like Baba hated me a little. And why not? After all, I *had* killed his beloved wife, his beautiful princess, hadn't I? The least I could have done was to have had the decency to have turned out a little more like him. (*The Kite Runner,* 17)

---

[3]Dr. Muzammil H. Siddiqi, "Why Does Allah Allow Suffering and Evil in the World?" *IslamOnline.net,* http://www.islamonline.net/servlet/Satellite?cid= 1119503544478&pagename=IslamOnline-English-Ask_Scholar/FatwaE/ FatwaEAskTheScholar.

[4]Leventry, "Why Bad Things Happen."

Many years passed before Amir learned the truth from Rahim Kahn. After the death of Ali, Hassan, and Baba, Amir alone remained to sort out his own sins and the sins of his father. But by this time Amir had learned to silence the gnawing guilt inside himself. Wrapped in layers of time and silence, he would need time to deal with the truth.

From the moment he witnessed the rape, Amir defined himself by his guilt. The book opens with, "I became what I am today at the age of twelve." He wasn't raped; Hassan was. But his failure to act left him stained with a spot much harder to remove than Hassan's blood that had spilled on the snow that day. He went through life with a secret sin, doubting his own worth or ability to be loved, seeing himself as less than others because of his sin and guilt. When Soraya confessed her past life to him before they became engaged, Amir thought:

> How could I, of all people, chastise someone for their past?...
>
> I envied her. Her secret was out. Spoken. Dealt with. I opened my mouth and almost told her how I'd betrayed Hassan, lied, driven him out, and destroyed a forty-year relationship between Baba and Ali. But I didn't. I suspected there were many ways in which Soraya Taheri was a better person than me. Courage was just one of them. (*The Kite Runner,* 144)

Fifteen years would pass before Amir would be able to tell his wife the truth.

Such doubts, fears, and guilt are common to humankind. In his *Letters and Papers from Prison,* Dietrich Bonhoeffer wrote, "Who am I? They mock me, these lonely questions of mine. Whoever I am, Thou knowest, O God, I am Thine!"[5] But since Amir was uncertain of God's existence, he couldn't even turn to God with the pain of his guilt.

Elizabeth O'Connor in *Cry Pain, Cry Hope* wrote about the layers people take on over time to protect themselves and the

---

[5]Dietrich Bonhoeffer, *Letters and Papers from Prison,* rev. ed. (New York: Macmillan, 1953), 221–22.

need to strip them away before God. She called this entry "The
Hulled Heart":

> Today in an early morning dream I was addressed by a
> voice. It asked, "What are you doing?" and I answered,
> "I am hulling my heart." The voice asked "Why?" and I
> answered, "I have need of a hulled heart."
>
> I awoke, as I have so often this year, knowing that
> in my sleep I was at work on my life, convinced that if I
> dug in its soil long enough, deep enough, it would yield
> me a liberating truth. Is that truth in the metaphor
> "hulled heart"? I think only of pulling off the green
> leaves of strawberries that the fruit may be eaten. But
> hulling means more than that. We strip corn and peas
> of husks and pods to reach the inner fruit. What are the
> hard, protective casings around my heart that must be
> stripped away to reach the hidden grain? What must I
> give up to lie all bare and exposed like peas in a pod or
> corn on a cob? What are the wrappings that keep the
> essence of life from becoming bread for the world? "This
> is my body broken for you. Eat you all of it."
>
> All this year old occupations have not had the same
> meaning. They are husks that wrap me too tight around.
> I want to throw them off in one grand gesture, but I am
> afraid of falling into the ground and dying. I am afraid
> of discarding the threadbare garments I huddle in for
> fear that I will stand cold and shivering in the dark,
> waiting for an angel that may not come. Nevertheless I
> am haunted by the biblical fact that it was the people
> who sat in darkness who saw a great light.[6]

Rahim Kahn's call sets Amir on a journey that will peel away
all his protective layers. By the end of the journey, he's no closer
to happily-ever-after than he was on the kite-fighting day when
he was twelve, but layer by layer he loses the weight of guilt
and finally discovers how it feels to find forgiveness.

When Sohrab tried to commit suicide by slitting his wrists,
Amir prayed while his nephew and only living blood relative

---

[6]Elizabeth O'Connor, *Cry Pain, Cry Hope* (Waco, Tex.: Word, 1987), 16.

lay in the balance between life and death. He asked God to forgive him that night, but it took more time for Amir to forgive himself:

> Sometime in the middle of the night, I slid out of bed and went to Sohrab's room. I stood over him, looking down, and saw something protruding from under his pillow. I picked it up. Saw it was Rahim Khan's Polaroid, the one I had given Sohrab the night we had sat by the Shah Faisal Mosque. The one of Hassan and Sohrab standing side by side, squinting in the light of the sun, and smiling like the world was a good and just place…
>
> I slipped the picture back where I had found it. Then I realized something: That last thought had brought no sting with it. Closing Sohrab's door, I wondered if that was how forgiveness budded, not with the fanfare of epiphany, but with pain gathering its things, packing up, and slipping away unannounced in the middle of the night. (*The Kite Runner,* 313)

We are assured of God's love and forgiveness if we only repent and believe: "Since all have sinned and fall short of the glory of God' they are now justified by his grace as a gift, through the redemption that is in Christ Jesus" (Rom. 3:23). "For the wages of sin is death, but the free gift of God is eternal life in Christ Jesus our Lord" (Rom. 6:23). "Everyone who believes in him receives forgiveness of sins through his name" (Acts 10:43).

But even with God's forgiveness, forgiving ourselves may be the hardest part. That was true for both Amir and for Sohrab. Sohrab's guilt is perhaps the saddest in the book. He felt dirty for the abuse his young body had taken from Asseph; and later he felt guilty for hurting his abuser, even to save the life of the one who sought to save him.

> "Will God…" he began, and choked a little. "Will God put me in hell for what I did to that man?"
>
> I reached for him and he flinched. I pulled back. "Nay. Of course not," I said. I wanted to pull him close, hold him, tell him the world had been unkind to him, not the other way around.

His face twisted and strained to stay composed. "Father used to say it's wrong to hurt even bad people. Because they don't know any better, and because bad people sometimes become good."...

"You saved my life in Kabul..."

He wiped his face with the sleeve of his shirt...He buried his face in his hands and wept a long time before he spoke again. "I miss Father, and Mother too," he croaked. "And I miss Sasa and Rahim Khan sahib. But sometimes I'm glad they're not...they're not here anymore."

"Why?" I touched his arm. He drew back.

"Because—" he said, gasping and hitching between sobs, "because I don't want them to see me...I'm so dirty." He sucked in his breath and let it out in a long, wheezy cry. "I'm so dirty and full of sin." (*The Kite Runner*, 277–78)

Amir tried to reassure Sohrab that he had been a victim, that he had committed no sin, but when Sohrab learned that on top of everything else he might have to go back to the orphanage, his pain was so great that he decided to end his life. And having lived through the suicide attempt, he told Amir that he wished he had let him die.

The book ends with the first ray of hope that Sohrab might begin to recover mentally, emotionally, physically, and spiritually. Amir has put all his energy into saving Sohrab, for in saving Sohrab Amir has learned that he is also saving himself.

Rahib Kahn had written about Baba in his final letter to Amir:

Sometimes I think everything he did, feeding the poor on the streets, building the orphanage, giving money to friends in need, it was all his way of redeeming himself. And that, I believe, is what true redemption is, Amir jan, when guilt leads to good.

I know that in the end, God will forgive. He will forgive your father, me, and you too. I hope you can do the same. Forgive your father if you can. Forgive me if you wish. But, most important, forgive yourself. (*The Kite Runner,* 263–64)

Amir finally forgave himself, turned his guilt into good, and found redemption.

In the movie *Pretty Woman,* Richard Gere is a wealthy, successful, but relationship-challenged businessman; and Julia Roberts is a young, intelligent prostitute who wants more out of life. The two of them fall in love during a week when Gere has hired her as an employee to be his date for the week, a step he believes will avoid relationship complications. As he sees himself through her eyes, he begins to change—though only so far. He offers her an apartment and lots of money, but she declines his offer because she says she wants romance. She'll wait for a knight in shining armor to rescue her and take her away. Finally Gere, following the advice of the hotel manager, realizes she is too valuable to let her go. He finds her and climbs up her fire escape to be her knight in shining armor and rescue her. Then he asks, "So what happens after he climbs up and rescues her?" And she answers, "She rescues him right back."

At the end of the book Amir and Sohrab are off on a journey to save each other, running free in the wind.

DISCUSSION QUESTIONS

---

1. In what ways are the commandments broken in *The Kite Runner*? Can they all be identified as theft?
2. Compare Christian and Muslim beliefs about suffering. In what ways do they differ? How are they alike?

CHAPTER 8

Living Life
"a Thousand Times Over"

"Hassan"' I called. "Come back with it"'
He was already turning the street corner, his rubber boots
kicking up snow. He stopped, turned. He cupped his hands
around his mouth. "For you a thousand times over!" he said.
Then he smiled his Hassan smile and disappeared around the
corner. The next time I saw him smile unabashedly like that was
twenty-six years later, in a faded Polaroid photograph.

(*The Kite Runner,* 59)

In the movie *Groundhog Day,* actor Bill Murray plays Phil
Connors, an arrogant weatherman on a TV station in Pittsburgh.
He's on assignment with his cameraman and producer in
Punxsutawney, Pennsylvania, for the annual Groundhog Day
celebration. Because of a blizzard, the team of three must spend
a second night in Punxsutawney, but when Phil gets up the next
morning it's Groundhog Day all over again—only no one but
Phil knows they are living the same day over and over again.

Phil has a chance to get one day absolutely right. He learns
to play the piano, speak French, make ice sculptures, and to do
lots of good deeds for the citizens of Punxsutawney. Along the
way, however, before he gets it right, he seduces women, steals
money and the groundhog, smokes, drinks, eats unhealthy food,
and commits suicide many times over—all because what he does
has no consequences. He does all the things some people think

they'd like to do if they could, if what they did had no ramifications. But Phil finds that a life of selfish indulgence isn't very rewarding. Somehow he'd missed this point living one day at a time, but by living the same day over and over again, Phil gradually realizes what it will take to do it right.

First, Phil tries to do some right things for the wrong reasons. He decides he likes Rita, the producer, played by Andie McDowell, so he pursues her. He drinks the drink she likes. He learns French poetry because she likes it. He tries to get her favorite foods. But he still does everything with a selfish motive, and it doesn't work.

Over time Phil changes. He develops a routine of helping people. Rita then sees him as a caring, well-liked, talented person, and she's attracted to him. He doesn't have to do anything to impress her but to be himself. Finally he gets it right and wakes up to a new day.

In the real world—even in most fiction—people don't live the same day over and over, but they do go through cycles trying to figure out what they're doing and why. Amir is a prime example.

All of his life Amir tries to get Baba's attention and to please him. Baba doesn't like Amir's interest in poetry, reading, and writing. He doesn't like his lack of aggression. When Baba builds the orphanage, Amir thinks those children are getting all of Baba's attention, so he tells Baba he has cancer. Baba doesn't even acknowledge him. He does get Baba's approval when he wins the kite-fighting contest, but because of his cowardice when Hassan is raped, his victory is never satisfying. In America Baba is pleased with Amir and affirms his educational progress. But now everything is tainted by Amir's big secret sin.

After the day of the kite-flying contest, Amir has another agenda. No longer is he focused on Baba alone. Now he must deal with his sin. His first response is more sin. First it's small, rude behavior, avoiding the living reminder of what he's done, or bullying Hassan. None of that works, so he weaves a web of sin to rid his life of Hassan forever. He succeeds in removing him physically, but the ghosts of the past are always present.

Over time the two problems combine. When Amir is called to Pakistan by Rahim Kahn and hears what he is being asked to do, Amir has a choice to make. He can let the old cowardice take over, proving once again in his own mind that Baba was right about him after all, or he can risk everything and get out of the spiral of guilt and fear.

> I wished Rahim Khan hadn't called me. I wished he had let me live on in my oblivion. But he had called me. And what Rahim Khan revealed to me changed things. Made me see how my entire life, long before the winter of 1975, dating back to when that singing Hazara woman was still nursing me, had been a cycle of lies, betrayals, and secrets.
> *There is a way to be good again,* he'd said.
> A way to end the cycle. (*The Kite Runner,* 198)

Amir's story is just one example of the nature of circular time in *The Kite Runner*. In dozens of ways, life keeps repeating itself: the parallel lives of Ali and Baba, Hassan and Amir, and even Assef and Amir. Life keeps coming back on itself in lots of ways. The contrasts, comparisons, and cycles of life represented in *The Kite Runner* prompt a closer look at time and how we measure it.

The Nature of Time

How time is viewed is cultural.[1] It can be viewed as linear or cyclical. The TV show *Sunday Morning* with Charles Osgood recently offered an example of these two perspectives. In one small segment Osgood read a few lines of rhyme about the "big bang" creating Earth, showing Earth from a perspective of space. It ended with the image morphing into a fingerprint, implying, to me, God's hand in creation as well as in the ongoing cycles of nature and life on Earth. Then came a segment about Kenny Rogers, a man with a string of award-winning songs and rejected wives. When asked about his past successes, Rogers answered, "I don't even remember those things. I only look to the future." One segment had a cyclical perspective of time; the other, a linear.

---

[1]"The Cultural Rhythms of Life," http://www.trinity.edu/~mkearl/time-c.html.

Such differences in looking at time are cultural. In *The Dance of Life*, Edward T. Hall wrote about the cultural rhythms of life.[2] Most people today live in structured environments. They create their own schedules rather than living by the natural rhythms of seasons and sun. Time relates to work hours, both our own and the businesses with whom we deal. We run our lives by schedules and deadlines. But even in our socially controlled way of measuring time, we find rhythms. And we mesh with the rhythms of our culture. Moving from one culture to another means an adjustment in the rhythms of time. For example, visiting Spain means dinner at ten o'clock at night and social activities until the morning hours, which then leads to the need for a siesta in the afternoon.

Hall distinguishes between monochronic time and poly-chronic time. Polychronic time focuses more on people and the completion of tasks than on schedules. Deadlines are less important than the journey, the process, the concerns of the individuals involved. Monochronic time is measured by mo-ments. Time is measured—spent, wasted, gained, lost, made up, killed, running out, moving in slow motion. Human needs are less important that keeping the schedules. These two ways of relating to time may clash. Individuals may be drawn to polychronic time while living in a monochronic world. Entire cultures can be more monochronic or polychronic, and in a world of cross-cultural business and social relationships, such differences may be difficult to overcome.

The differences, however, go deeper. Some cultures see history as linear; others see it as cyclical. Does history repeat itself? Or is it always progressive? Are those who don't learn from history destined to repeat it? Or should businesses and governments focus only on the present and future? A cyclical perspective means that individuals and entire cultures periodi-cally have another chance to deal with an issue and perhaps to do a better job than they did the first time. In linear time each event is new and presents a one-time chance to do something well or poorly.

---

[2]Edward T. Hall, *The Dance of Life: The Other Dimension of Time* (Garden City, N.Y.: Anchor Press/ Doubleday, 1983).

The immediacy of the postmodern world creates a fascination with time. Moving from one year to the next may mean that to be accurate atomic clocks must readjust by fractions of a second. Individuals want what they want when they want it with little patience for waiting, planning for a future payoff, or delayed gratification. For example, people in linear, monochronic societies don't save well; they seldom take on projects that may take generations to complete, such as building a great cathedral; in fact, they have difficulty maintaining their infrastructure (such as levees) until the need is immediate; and they're never without a watch. Gandhi said there is more to life than increasing its speed.

Western societies tend to be more linear and monochronic; Eastern cultures tend to be more cyclical and polychronic. An Eastern orientation is evident in *The Kite Runner*. The characters go through cycles of opportunities to deal with the same issues in their lives. Amir has more than one opportunity to deal with pleasing his father, finding courage, dealing with his sin and guilt, and finding forgiveness and redemption. He finally gets it right but in doing so simply continues the cycle of life that now includes another generation.

We see the same kinds of cycles in the Old Testament stories of the patriarchs. The promise moves from generation to generation, from Abraham to Isaac to Jacob. Four hundred years later Moses moves the Hebrew people out of Egypt and toward the promised land, but even then the people doubt God's ability to lead them, and they spend another forty years in the wilderness before the next generation gets another chance to cross the river and enter the land God promised. Believers today enter the same cycle of seeking to follow God, messing up, trying again to do it right, and passing the hope and promise of redemption on to the next generation. Every person in every generation can learn from the past but must choose to enter into relationship with God and continue the cycle of temptation, sin, guilt, repentance, forgiveness, and redemption. Each person, though growing as a believer, may move through this process many times.

Salvation, then, is less easily understood in linear time than in cyclical time. It is less a one-time event, though it is that, and more of an ongoing process: we have been saved, we are being saved, we will be saved. Christians were saved, first of all by Jesus' redemptive act on the cross and then by their own individual decision to follow him. We are being saved daily as we relate to God through our opportunities to serve him and others on our life's journey. We will be saved at death when we step into eternity.

Kenneth S. Wuest, in his expanded translation of the New Testament, helps non-Greek readers capture this ongoing nature of time in the perfect tense of Greek verbs. For example, in Ephesians 2:8-10, the NRSV reads, "For by grace you have been saved through faith, and this is not your own doing; it is the gift of God—not the result of works, so that no one may boast. For we are what he has made us, created in Christ Jesus for good works, which God prepared beforehand to be our way of life." The same passage in the Wuest translation begins: "For by grace have you been saved in time past completely, through faith, with the result that your salvation persists through present time."[3] It may not read as lyrically, but it reminds us of action ongoing.

This is the nature of sacred time. Sacred time allows us—as Westerners caught up in the busyness of a monochronic, linear culture—to pull out of that kind of time to focus on people and their needs, and to enter into the cyclical nature of sacred time, joining with God followers of all generations:

> Now faith is the assurance of things hoped for, the conviction of things not seen. Indeed by faith our ancestors received approval. By faith we understand that the worlds were prepared by the word of God, so that what is seen was made from things that are not visible...

> By faith Abraham obeyed when he was called to set out for a place that he was to receive as an inheritance; and he set out, not knowing where he was going...By faith Moses...By faith the people...By faith Rahab the prostitute...

---

[3]Kenneth S. Wuest, *The New Testament: An Expanded Translation* (Grand Rapids, Mich.: Eerdmans, 1961), 451.

Time would fail me to tell of Gideon, Barak, Samson, Jephthah, of David and Samuel and the prophets…

Therefore, since we are surrounded by so great a cloud of witnesses, let us also lay aside every weight and the sin that clings so closely, and let us run with perseverance the race that is set before us. (Heb. 11:1–3, 8, 23, 29, 31, 32; 12:1)

Like Amir, we can run free from guilt, feeling the wind of God's blessing on us and hope and promise for a new generation.

DISCUSSION QUESTIONS

1. Amir can't go back in time to correct his mistakes, but he can make a difference in the next generation. Which is better, to try to make past wrongs right or just to go about doing good in an attempt to be a positive force in the world?

2. Is it ever too late in life to become what you at some point in your past aspired to become?

3. Which is more harmful, living in the past or ignoring it?

4. Who usually suffers most from a person's guilt? Why and in what ways?

APPENDIX: Online Resources

Kites

http://coda.co.za/kites_and_kite_flying/history.htm
http://www.gombergkites.com/nkm/hist1.html
http://www.skratch-pad.com/kites/where.html
http://www.users.voicenet.com/~foster/kites/page2.htm
http://www.funattic.com/kite_history.htm
http://www.afghana.com/Entertainment/Gudiparanbazi.htm
http://origin.dailynews.lk/2002/01/22/wor03.html
http://www.rferl.org/features/2002/11/15112002192521.asp
http://www.lcl.lib.ne.us/INFO/obol/obol2005/obol2005-2.htm
http://www.the-south-asian.com/June2002/Baba_Saheb_ Kite_
aficionado.htm
http://www.travel-wise.com/asia/malaysia2/moonkite/index.html
http://www.art.unt.edu/offlinentieva/artcurr/japan/kites.htm

Afghanistan

http://www.cia.gov/cia/publications/factbook/geos/af.html http://
www.imb.org/CompassionNetPeopleGroupResults.asp?Hitdate2=
Currentdatetime%28%29&PrayerCode=24008&Age=90&submit12=
Find+ Prayer+Items (brief information about Christians came from
this site)
http://www.afghan-web.com/facts.html
http://www.afghangoverment.com/briefhistory.htm
http://www.afghanmagazine.com/2004_06/articles/hsadat.shtml
http://www.gmc.edu/library/kite_runner.htm
http://www.afghana.com/culture
http://www.asia.msu.edu/centralasia/Afghanistan/culture.html

Islam

http://www.afghan-network.net/Islam/
http://www.islamicity.com/Mosque/ihame/Ref2.htm
http://islam.about.com/library/weekly/aa120298.htm
http://www.adherents.com/Religions_By_Adherents.html (statistics)
http://www.bbc.co.uk/religion/religions/islam/beliefs/index.shtml
http://www.religioustolerance.org/isl_intr1.htm